FINDING MY SELF

FINDING MY SELF

A Life in Education and Activism

Chand Kishore Saint

Orient BlackSwan

FINDING MY SELF: A LIFE IN EDUCATION AND ACTIVISM

ORIENT BLACKSWAN PRIVATE LIMITED

Registered Office
3-6-752 Himayatnagar, Hyderabad 500 029, Telangana, India
e-mail: centraloffice@orientblackswan.com

Other Offices
Bengaluru, Chennai, Guwahati, Hyderabad, Kolkata,
Mumbai, New Delhi, Noida, Patna, Visakhapatnam

© Orient Blackswan Private Limited 2023
First published by Orient Blackswan Private Limited 2023

ISBN 978-93-5442-467-0

Typeset in
Plantin Std 11/13.75
by Le Studio Graphique, Gurgaon 122 007

Printed in India at
Thomson Press, New Delhi 110 020

Published by
Orient Blackswan Private Limited
3-6-752 Himayatnagar, Hyderabad 500 029, Telangana, India
e-mail: info@orientblackswan.com

Contents

Acknowledgements

Chand Kishore Saint (1932–2022) passed away on 15 August 2022, a few months before his 90th birthday, mourned by family and a host of friends, former students and well-wishers in educational institutions and the voluntary sector across Rajasthan, India and the wider world, which he had been part of and contributed so much to. Sadly, he was unable to see though the editorial process for this memoir, although the manuscript had been accepted for publication in his lifetime.

We are sure that he would have been keen to acknowledge the many friends, colleagues and relatives who helped ensure this story reached completion. On his behalf, with the realisation that this list may be incomplete, we would like to mention in particular the generosity of spirit and kindness of Alok Bhalla, who read through an early draft and provided incisive comments, besides translating key passages from Hindi during editing. Thanks to Mackenzie Shreve, who helped immeasurably in transcribing the first part of the book in electronic form, as well as Mihir, for being there. Ajay Mehta, Ashish Kothari, Aseem Srivastava, Tejbir Singh, Ashis Nandy, E. P. Menon, David Goldman, Ashoke Chatterjee, Keshav, Vishnu Sharma, Ginny Srivastava, Rita Dixit, Mannaram Dangi, Ronak Shah, Nilima Khaitan, and the extended network of NGOs in Udaipur were a source of intellectual sustenance, encouragement and support in the difficult last phase, especially the crisis-ridden Covid-19 years. We appreciate the affection and care extended by close friends—the late Suresh Amonkar, his son Raj and the Goa family, as well as the late Chandrasekhar Sastry and the family in Bangalore, storytellers all.

Ubeshwar Vikas Mandal staff, especially Kesuji Kuria, have been a bulwark and mainstay through times of crisis. The interactions with the community live on in memory and in stories that will undoubtedly continue to be told.

Many thanks to Ashok Upadhyaya and *The Beacon* magazine for carrying an earlier version of an excerpt of my father's and uncle's account of the educational experience in Kenya.[1]

Thanks to Shikshantar, especially Manish Jain, and the Long and Winding Road Programme, Centre for Education and Documentation, for videotaped interviews that allowed my father to share his early formative experiences (including the influence of his great-grandmother's storytelling abilities and the traumatic events of the 1947 Partition).[2]

We would like to acknowledge the meticulous editorial work by the team at Orient BlackSwan, especially Sanna Jain.

A special note of thanks to my uncle Prem Saint in California, for his careful reading of the edits and responses, to my sister Amita Arya and family in London, and my mother Sudesh Saint, for their unstinting support in this endeavour.

Thanks to Amita Arya for the cover drawing and to Mishta Roy for the cover design.

Tarun K. Saint
July 2023

ENDNOTES

1. See 'Memories are Made of This!', available at https://www.thebeacon.in/2021/07/30/memories-are-made-of-this-africa-on-my-mind/ (accessed 29 June 2023).

2. See 'The Making of Kishore Saint: As Told by Him Five Years before He Passed', available at https://www.youtube.com/watch?v=QnD1KajyMgI (accessed 29 June 2023). See also 'Thoughts on Hind Swaraj: Kishore Saint', available at https://www.youtube.com/watch?v=P0BgzvKgfY8 accessed (29 June 2023).

Preface

The Purpose and Scope of
Writing these Memoirs

The writing of these memoirs began as a response to my
family members, who urged me to leave a record of
my life lived across four continents, over eight decades of
the twentieth and twenty-first centuries. However, as the
memories unfolded, questions arose about the purpose of
writing memoirs beyond the interest of family, especially
with regard to my involvement in public work. These were
reinforced by younger friends and erstwhile colleagues, who
were interested in learning from my experience and reflection.
My interest in Gandhi led me to his autobiography, *The Story
of My Experiments with Truth*. This inspired me to treat the
writing of these memoirs as a means to self-understanding,
self-recovery and self-correction.

As I prepared to write, the question arose of where to
start. Although my earliest memories are of events that
occurred when I was four years old, I decided to begin these
memoirs by writing about my life after my arrival in Kenya,
having migrated from India with my brother and great-
grandmother. That was when I took up my first job as a clerk
in a shipping company. This was followed by my becoming
an assistant master at a school and discovering my vocation
as a teacher. In this capacity, I availed of opportunities for
higher education and professional training. After nearly two
decades of structured teaching and teacher education in
government service in Kenya, I decided to move into open-
ended, experimental and self-designed modes of education
and learning with the Friends World College in New York.

This was an interlude, a detour before returning to India for good to engage full-time in service to community and country through voluntary organisations, as well as independently. What follows are my reminiscences of my life and work in these various phases.

1

Kenya

1949–53

My first job was as an apprentice clerk in a British shipping company (Smith Mackenzie & Co. Ltd) in Mombasa, the main port of Kenya, which in 1949 was a British colony. I had arrived there in May 1949 as a refugee with my brother, Prem Kishore, and our great-grandmother or *Beji*, Mishrani Isher Devi. We were there to join our father, Dina Nath Saint, who had migrated from Punjab in 1946 to work as the headmaster of Sanatan Dharma School, a private Asian girls' school in Nairobi, the capital of Kenya. In 1948, he joined the Kenyan government service as a teacher in Allidina Visram High School in Mombasa. As an educator with literary and religious interests and a good command over English, he had already come to know important people from different communities. It was through one such acquaintance, Mr B. B. Austin, a Parsi from Bombay who worked as an office superintendent, that he arranged for me to begin working under Mr Austin's direct guidance with a desk in his office. Since I had no previous experience of, nor the required skills for, office work, I had to learn everything—typing, stenography, filing, despatch, book-keeping—from scratch. I bought self-instruction manuals to learn Pitman's shorthand and typing on a Remington typewriter. I would arrive in the office an hour before official time and practice the exercises on the typewriter. When Mr Austin arrived, usually early, he'd dictate to me simple letters and show me the setting for typing these on letterheads. A colleague, Ramzanali, an Asian from the Shia Muslim Ithna Ishri community, was charged to show me how to make voucher entries in the cashbook and ledgers, and how to carry out letter despatch work. All this had to be done meticulously as the superior British officers were very strict about how office work was done.

The offices of Smith Mackenzie and Co. were housed in a large double-storey building on a rise overlooking Kilindini Harbour. The ground floor had spacious, high-ceilinged godowns where goods were stored for import and export purposes. The workers there were Asian clerks and African porters. The administrative offices were on the first floor with strict segregation between the eastern and western sections. The eastern side had the offices of senior British officials, while the western side had a large room where Asian clerks and supervisors sat for accounts and record maintenance. A wide corridor ran along the length of the building, from east to west. The only African members of staff were office boys dressed in long white tunics and red Fez caps. They carried files from one office to another and twice a day prepared and served tea to the staff. The British officials seldom came to the clerical section. The only exception was an old lady. Every hour or so she emerged from her office and walked along the corridor, past our desks, to the balcony overlooking the main Kilindini road. She usually looked distracted, sometimes muttering to herself. For the Asian and African staff, she was a mystery. We never talked about her in our conversations during lunch break, but privately all of us had some idea about her. I used to think of her as the whale in Hermann Melville's *Moby Dick*, occasionally surfacing from the depths of the ocean to breathe fresh air. The only Asian who had access to the British officers was Mr Austin, through whom all communication between the officers and clerks was channelled.

I worked there for six months. During this time I was able to learn the basic office routines and skills, which helped me in my next job as a clerk in the primary school where my father had been appointed as headmaster. It was he who, in January 1950, arranged this appointment for me in the Kenyan government service, where I was to continue in various capacities till 1968. Majengo Primary School was only for Asians. In colonial Kenya, there was strict segregation in education, health facilities, housing and jobs along racial—European, Asian, African—lines. There was a clear hierarchy in terms of the quality of facilities and nature of jobs available. The best jobs were reserved for Europeans, who were almost all British. The middle-level clerical, trade and artisanal/technical jobs were reserved for Asians and the menial, unskilled manual labour was reserved for Africans. Similarly, the best education, health and housing facilities were for Europeans, mid-level for Asians and the most meagre for Africans. Many Asian families from Punjab were the descendants of builders of the railway line from Mombasa to Uganda, and were in the railway service.

The primary school I took up work in was located in an area that had both Asian private housing and commercial establishments clustered together, and comprised Gujarati, Punjabi Hindu and Sikh, and Khoja Muslim families. It was adjacent to two places of worship: the Arya Samaj and a Sikh Gurudwara. The school was a single-storey building built around a quadrilateral, with classrooms on all four sides and the headmaster's office at one corner. My office was next to the headmaster's. The school had 300 or so pupils studying from Standards One to Seven. Each class would have 40 to 50 pupils from different Asian communities, who were all keen to get their children educated for better career opportunities. There was a teaching staff of 10 or so and myself as a clerk. My tasks were to maintain records, do typing and despatch work, collect fees and dispense salaries, keep basic accounts and do bank transactions. Much of this I had to learn on the job, often with harsh and strict instruction from my father, the headmaster. He was well-known and feared for being a strict disciplinarian. Since the school was co-educational, with a large number of adolescent boys and girls in the upper classes, my father's demeanour in school was stricter than usual. He frowned upon any intermixing between boys and girls outside classes. Several times a day, he would take a round of the school along the corridors to ensure that every class was engaged in its proper work. Occasionally, when a teacher was absent, he would ask me to supervise a class or do some reading. I did not do any teaching, although I had obtained the basic qualification, having passed the matriculation and intermediate science examinations at Punjab University before coming to Kenya.

My work as a clerk in this school lasted only one year. In January 1951, the school was merged with Mbheni Primary School and shifted to new buildings in a different, more open and spacious institutional locality in Mombasa. That is where I began my teaching career in the primary classes, and where I discovered my vocation as an educator.

Mbheni Primary School was a three-storeyed concrete structure with a simple functional design of three classroom wings connected at a right angle with an administrative block. Since it was a new set-up, there was only the bare minimum furniture and equipment. Everything had to be arranged from scratch. The staff, some brought in from the earlier units and others newly recruited, had to be knit together afresh as a team. The headmaster, Mr Mallick, was an experienced hand on the verge of retirement. His deputy, Bhag Singh, was also in his 50s. Both were Punjabi, one Muslim and the other Sikh, but they shared a good rapport. Most of the teaching staff comprised young Punjabi men and women. I was one of the youngest. Being the son of a teacher who was a respected figure in both the community and the profession, I was soon given leadership responsibilities and administrative tasks, such as preparing the timetable. This was in addition to my main teaching work as an assistant master, for which I had to take classes in different subjects. Not having had any training as a teacher, I had to prepare my lessons with guidance from my father.

This was a period of rapid expansion in education facilities for Asians in Kenya, spurred on by greater demand from the community after the independence of India and Pakistan, as well as by a more enlightened educational policy of the British government in post-World War II Britain. This improvement was in both quantity and quality. A teacher training college for Asians was set up in the same institutional complex where in-service courses were started for teachers. After a year's work in Mbheni Primary School, I was selected for a six-month teacher training course. Here, I had the opportunity to work and learn under Miss Jean Walker, a specialist in early primary school teaching from the UK. I was given charge of a demonstration class held once a week in the college. The approach was based on a fun and play activity method of learning for children. I soon realised how enjoyable and creative it could be to play with and teach 5- and 6-year-olds. Under experienced guidance, I discovered my penchant for reaching out to children and young persons in order to help them to acquire new knowledge and come into their own. In addition to this special segment of training, we had courses in English language and literature, the study of nature, mathematics and history as subjects, teaching methods related to these, and basic/introductory knowledge of educational psychology, child development and various approaches to school education.

After this training, I returned to Mbheni Primary School and continued to teach in the First Standard class that I had taken for demonstration with Miss Walker. This position was a source of both envy and disdain amongst some of my colleagues—envy for the special attention given to this class for demonstration and as an example, and disdain for my teaching a lower class in terms of the status and qualifications required. This never discouraged me and I continued to derive satisfaction from the joyful learning and growth of children. My sentiment was vindicated recently when one of my students, Yunus Bagha, now a grandfather living in Canada, got in touch and told me about his vivid memories of that year—the stories and nursery rhymes, the games and the happy, caring atmosphere in the class. He has been calling me and we have talked on the phone: '*Pyare Master ji, aap se baat karke mujhe bahut sukoon milta hai*' ('Dear Teacher, I find great peace in talking to you'). This living voice of appreciation and gratitude, coming 65 years later with echoes of past remembrance, is the best reward a teacher can receive in her/his lifetime.

Together with teaching, I—along with others—took responsibility for the school timetable, boy scouts, first aid and basic training with the Red Cross unit in school, and other extracurricular activities. As a lively group of young staff, we also had our moments of relaxation, when we sang Hindi film songs, led by one of the Nath brothers. He had recently migrated from India and had a good singing voice. Rhythmic accompaniment was provided by some of us with *tabla* beats on classroom desks.

Goaded on and guided by my father, I took up private studies to prepare for the London matriculation examination. My brother Prem had also reached the upper secondary class and was studying in Allidina Visram High School, where my father had joined as a teacher. Father, whose ambition to study in England had been thwarted in the depressed 1930s, was keen that his sons should have this opportunity. Together with course work, we had plenty of reading material—magazines we subscribed to, books from father's collection and from libraries. These were all in English as that was the medium of instruction at higher levels of education and the means of communication for official work in colonial Kenya. Proficiency in speaking, reading and writing English was considered an asset in getting ahead in one's studies and career. To my surprise, I passed the matriculation exam in the first division; earlier in India, I had not done so well in the matriculation and intermediate examinations of Punjab University, missing the first division by 12 marks in matriculation and by one mark in the intermediate science exams.

Encouraged by this success—and armed now with the necessary qualification—I applied for higher studies in England under a government scholarship scheme for Asian teachers. Even though one felt inwardly excited at the prospect of study in England, there was not much hope of this materialising, since the competition was likely to be strong for the three scholarships announced that year. There was also the diffidence that came from living away from the capital Nairobi, in a place where applicants were likely to be smarter and well-connected to decision-makers.

Meanwhile, our life continued with its routines: getting ready early for the start of school at 8.00 AM, returning home at 12 noon for lunch and rest, back to school from 2.00 to 5.00 PM, and after a snack at home, off to the Railways Asian Club for recreation. The club had facilities for sports—football, hockey, cricket, table tennis, tennis and badminton. I tried my hand at all of these except tennis, and made some progress with the help of manuals that offered basic instructions for improving one's skills. For older persons, there were tables for cards and chess and carrom, where Father joined others to play bridge and chess. For a few months, I too joined early morning (6.00 AM) sessions of the Bhartiya Swayamsevak Sangh (BSS) *shakha* (as the Rashtriya Swayamsevak Sangh, or RSS, was renamed in Kenya) held at an open ground in the neighbourhood. The RSS had been banned in India after it was suspected of having played a role in Mahatma Gandhi's assassination. The ban was revoked after a couple of years and it began to function again openly.

The sessions began with the planting of the Hindu saffron flag, followed by a prayer song to Mother India, physical yogic exercises like Surya Namaskar, practising martial art skills with a staff, and instruction in Hindutva ideology. I quickly gained recognition and leadership and was put in charge of the shakha. On one special occasion, perhaps the Dussehra annual function, I was selected to sing a patriotic song praising the founder of the RSS. It was a large gathering of *swayamsevak*s (volunteers) and organisers. I was quite nervous when my name was called. In my enthusiasm, I ran to the front of the gathering. As I faced the microphone, I was breathing rapidly. I started to sing but could not control my voice, and the performance had to be curtailed midway. The shame and humiliation of this failure did not leave me for a long time, since I had practised the song for many days in solitude. Not long after I became disillusioned with the fanatic and authoritarian atmosphere of the organisation and stopped attending the shakha.

Asians in Kenya, as migrants and as segregated communities, had been able to preserve their social and cultural life and had adapted to the local circumstances. With our father's eclectic interests and initiatives, we partook of this in various ways. We were roped in to perform in dramatised episodes from the epics at Hindu religious festivals. We accompanied him to Urdu poetry recitals of Bazm-e-Adab, a group of Muslim, Hindu and Sikh Asians interested in Urdu literature. He also took us to classical music evenings hosted by Asian businessmen with local and visiting singers and instrumentalists. As a Theosophist, he was invited to speak on religions at different religious gatherings. I went to some of these, often overwhelmed by the flow and command of his speech, though much of its meaning was beyond me. As a teacher, Father was also invited to meals by the families of some of his students. He usually took us along. These were always warm occasions, with effulgent Indian hospitality on full display. Through these, we were introduced to the rich Gujarati and Sindhi cuisine and language. In my case, with Beji by then in her 80s, some of these occasions were intended for indirect probing prior to proposals for my marriage. This was given serious consideration in view of Beji's advanced age and the need for a 'bahu' to take charge of housekeeping. However, I was not ready for this.

Away from this rich community life and fulfilling work at school, I would cycle or walk to the seafront near Fort Jesus, a relic from Mombasa's Portuguese past, now a museum and archaeological site. I'd sit for hours listening to the wind whistling through casuarina pines and the waves breaking against the raised coral reefs jutting out to the sea. I would gaze for long at the vast Indian Ocean to the east with occasional steamships and windblown dhows passing by. At low tide, tangled branches of mangrove trees would appear along the shore. In this solace and solitude I'd burst into song, laden with sadness and yearning, for what I knew not. In some strange way, this would relieve the tensions of living in a cramped household with an asthmatic, often angry father, burdened by memories of his early widowhood, a failed second marriage, the sacrifices he had made for us by leaving that behind and his expectations from me to 'settle down'. During particularly severe bouts of asthma, he would feel as though he was on the verge of death. He would call us to sit and watch his agony, which we did, sobbing and crying. Eventually the 'attack' would subside and he'd go to sleep, allowing us to slip away.

Living through this agony of a home and ecstasy at school and oft in communion with nature, I had almost forgotten the application I had sent in for a scholarship to study in England. One day a letter came from the Ministry of Education in Nairobi with the message that I had been shortlisted as a candidate and should reach Nairobi for an interview, scheduled for March or April 1952. This came as a surprise.

Growing up as a child indifferently cared for by relatives, I had learnt to shun any ambition or high expectations and to accept whatever came my way. So this call took some time to sink in. At home, there was a mixed response from father. He was pleased that a window of opportunity had opened up for me to move ahead in my career, but was dismayed that moves for my marriage had to be abandoned. There was also the worry that I would be spoiled, become anglicised and neglect the family. Beji, of course, was distraught to learn that she would not have a bahu at home soon, and may not live long enough to welcome one.

Amongst the few colleagues who came to know about this, there was a mixture of admiration and envy. In the end, it was left to me to decide. There was some trepidation and fear on my part, but finally, the desire to be free, on my own in the unknown, prevailed and I decided to go for the interview. Suitable clothing for colder weather in Nairobi and a necktie as a formal necessity were purchased. Father gave me some tips and practice in facing interviews with British officials. Largely, it was left to my own imagination and luck.

I reached Nairobi by overnight train in a sleeper compartment for Asians. Bedding and meals, including bed tea in the morning, were provided. This was my first experience of travelling alone in Kenya. In Nairobi, it was a cold day with a cloudy sky and occasional drizzle. I arrived at the Ministry of Education early and was led to an upper floor. A few other candidates were already there in the corridor. I knew no one and there was no effort to talk to each other. Everyone looked anxious, waiting to be called. When it was my turn, I was ushered into a small room with a large desk. Four education officers, three British and one Asian, sat behind the desk. I was asked to sit on a chair facing them. I have no recollection of the course the interview took. There is only a hazy picture in my mind of the dimly lit office, their stern white faces and a not-too-sympathetic tall Asian personage. A few questions were asked, to which I muttered some answers. It lasted only a few minutes, with me in a semi-dazed state. As I came out, dismayed at having failed to rise to the occasion, another candidate, a tall Goan with a trimmed mustache and thick-rimmed glasses, sensed my gloom. He came forward to console me with a kindly smile. I found out later that he was Neves Pereira, who was to become my best friend and like an elder brother to me. The next day, I took the train back to Mombasa.

I walked home to Makupa from the railway station as there was no local transport on that route. Later, when I was preparing my claim for travel to and from Nairobi, Father asked me to include an amount for local travel. I refused to do this as I had not incurred any such expense. He was not too pleased, but let it be. I had taken a stand to always be truthful, as we were constantly told to be at home and in school. In practice, such claims were made according to provisions in the rules and were considered entitlements. I could have done so, but I felt that only claiming expenses that had been actually incurred was the right thing to do. I have adhered to this principle and practice in my work with various institutions.

In the months following the interview, my life settled back into the routines of school, home and community. I had given up any hope of being selected after my perceived 'failure' in the interview. Even the talk of marriage was revived, and Beji began to look forward to a bahu. However, in July–August we received a message that I had been selected for the scholarship and efforts were being made to get me admitted in a college/university in England. This changed everything. It shook me out of my stupor of being resigned to a modest, secure job as an assistant master, dutifully supporting my family as the oldest in my generation. Once again the excitement of a new life opening up took hold of me. Colleagues began to treat me with new respect, boosting my self-perception and confidence. Father and my brother Prem both expressed (and felt) a sense of pride that at last, someone in the family had the opportunity of going to England for study, thus fulfilling a dream that had been nurtured over generations. But for Beji, our guardian angel, it was a hard blow, as she had to abandon her last hope for a bahu in the family. She increasingly withdrew into herself with her deities and recitations from the *Bhagawad Gita,* turning her *mala* (rosary) with holy mantras and fasting. Her health began to fail and she passed on into the world of her Ishta in December 1952. I felt guilty about all this, but bore it with a sense of detachment.

As it turned out, getting admission in a college/university in England was not a straightforward task. Though I had matriculated from London University and passed the Faculty of Science Intermediate examination of Punjab University, this was not enough for admission to a degree course. The Punjab University qualification was not recognised in England. I'd have to pass an equivalent examination from a British University. This meant that my studies would require four years and the three-year scholarship would have to be extended. Finally, a solution was found for my admission to University College in Hull. This was still a college affiliated to London University, where I could spend the first year preparing for the intermediate examination of that university and qualify for a degree course. I chose biology, chemistry and physics as I had already studied these at Punjab University. Subsequently, for my degree course, I chose geography, with geology as my subsidiary, for a Bachelor of Science (Honours) degree. I did not know all these intricacies at the time. I learnt this later in England from my tutor at Hull, Professor Brachi, who also told me that the Kenyan government had almost given up on my case. A way forward was found through his personal intervention.

After my admission was confirmed, preparations began to equip me for the journey and a new life away from home. Warm clothing was arranged with some difficulty. In Mombasa, with its warm climate throughout the year, clothes shops did not stock woollens. So jackets and trousers of thick cotton cloth had to be tailored. For travel documents, a new passport had to be arranged. I had come to Kenya after India's independence on an Indian passport. However, my father, who had migrated in 1946, was a British subject. He arranged for my brother and I to be registered as British subjects, with British passports as citizens of the UK and colonies. To prepare us for life in England, the British Council arranged a three-week residential course as our orientation. This was held at Jeanes School, a training facility for athletes, 30 miles west of Nairobi in Kenya's highlands. There we were shown how to make beds, to use cutlery, to use Western-style flush toilets, to dress appropriately for different occasions and to maintain etiquette and good manners. We were also introduced to three-course English meals with soup, main dish and a sweet, in that order. Meal times—bed tea, breakfast, lunch, afternoon tea, supper, high tea, dinner—were also explained. In addition, there were lectures on various aspects of British life. I have no recollection of their contents as it was difficult for me to comprehend them due to the accents of the speakers.

After the course, there was a period of waiting during which I finished my work at school. There were also some farewell invitations from families whose children I had taught, as well as functions at school and in the community. Travel was arranged by the Ministry of Education. In October 1953, I left Mombasa by train for Nairobi, seen off at the station by friends, family and colleagues. From Nairobi, along with Neves Pereira and Atiq Qureshi, the other two students selected that year, we took the British Overseas Airways Corporation (BOAC) flight for a 15-hour journey to London via Cairo.

Departure from Kenya brought to a close my transition from adolescence to adulthood, marked by family tensions and partially fulfilled expectations, relieved by my youthful excitement in beginning a career as a teacher. It also marked the move from a colonial, segregated society to the Empire's homeland, where I would be given opportunities for learning and growth among my peers.

2

England

1953–58

We were received at London airport by British Council officials and taken to East Africa House, a hostel for students from Kenya, Tanganyika (part of present-day Tanzania) and Uganda. Each of us had a room of our own with a heater for warmth. However, London in autumn was quite cold for us from the tropics. As my clothing was totally inadequate for this weather, we were taken to Burtons, a readymade clothing store on Oxford Street. There I bought my first woollen tweed jacket and trousers and a winter overcoat, using the clothing allowance given to us in British currency.

We had to stay there for two weeks as the new term in the college began in late October. During this time we explored the streets and landmarks in the West End of London—Oxford Street, Regent Street, Piccadilly, Bond Street, Hyde Park, Trafalgar Square, Houses of Parliament, The Mall. These names were familiar from the game of Monopoly we had played as children and from our English literature and civics textbooks in school. We also saw the remnants of some sites that had been bombed during World War II. We sometimes took buses or the Tube, but usually we just walked. It was a time of acclimatisation and learning, combined with exhilaration and wonder at the new world we had come to. In the hostel we were served only English meals with fixed portions. In post-war Britain, rationing was still in force. This took some getting used to and we were often hungry. With our modest allowances, we could not afford to eat in restaurants. Working women from East End served food and did the housekeeping. We were often unable to follow their London Cockney accents, but they were always kind, jovial and considerate, putting us at our ease at the dining table.

At the end of two weeks Atiq and I were put on the train to Hull at Kings Cross station. It was a day-long journey from south to north, traversing the lush, green English countryside with its low hills, dales and plains, broken by mining and industrial towns, a landscape I got to know and understand better through my studies in geography and geology.

At Hull we were received by a member of college staff and taken to Camp Hall in Cottingham, a large village 7 miles west of Hull. There we met Mr Treherne, the resident warden of the hostel. I lived there for the next two years. Camp Hall was a US Army Camp dating back to World War II. It had Nissan huts—15-foot high, semi-cylindrical structures with corrugated iron sheets stretched over four rooms measuring 8 by 10 feet, with a common corridor and toilet and bathroom, all enclosed within single brick walls. Each room had a single bed, chair, writing table with a small bookshelf, a cupboard, wardrobe and an electric heater. Even by the standards of post-war Britain, it was a spartan facility. The other two hostels of the college, Ferens Hall and Thwaite Hall, were modern brick buildings with central heating, spacious rooms and better facilities. Rooms were allotted to women students in Thwaite Hall and to men students in senior years in Ferens Hall, with preference given to those with better academic performance. There were four of us in the Nissan Hut where I was allotted a room. Three of them were English from different counties, each with his own accent. It took me several months to make sense of what they were saying.

The dining room was about 200 yards away from our hut. There were set times for meals and fixed quantities of food due to rationing. Evening meals and lunch on holidays were eaten together in the presence of the hostel warden, who led the prayer before the meal. Basic English fare was served with some variations, including a meat dish, except on Fridays when fish was served instead of meat. Bread and butter were made available for a late evening snack. We toasted these on an electric heater in the room after finishing our evening studies. Sometimes we took a walk to the Cottingham Village fish and chips shop to relish fried fish and chips, served wrapped in a newspaper sheet. At formal evening dinners, there was a high table where the warden and lecturers sat with the students who were invited to join them. The tables nearest the high table were for senior students, while the freshers sat at the table furthest from the high table. Thus, there was a well-established hierarchy with little informal interaction between senior and junior year students. For us newcomers from the colonies, it was not easy to be accepted in this hierarchy. Most of us kept to ourselves. There were also bouts of homesickness; then Atiq and I would get together in my room and, using the heater as a *tabla*/drum, we would sing Hindi film songs, much to the amusement of our English companions in the adjacent rooms.

When the term began, our whole routine changed. We had to get up early to be ready to catch the bus or cycle from the hostel to the college 5 miles away. Classes began at 9.00 AM and went on till 1.00 PM. Afternoons were free for sports, both indoors and outdoors. We returned to the hostel after 5.00 PM for supper/high tea, following which we studied in our rooms or in the library. During the first couple of weeks, there were special events. A dinner, followed by a ballroom dance, was arranged for freshers. This included an address by the Principal, Nicholson, who welcomed the new entrants and stressed that the ethos of the college was that of a community of scholars, where everyone was expected to contribute to community life through active participation in sports, and cultural and academic clubs. These were run by the student management, under the aegis of the student union with its own elected executive committee. I listened to this with close attention, at once feeling included amongst strangers in a land far away from home. With this experience my nostalgia for home vanished. Atiq and I stood around for a while when the ballroom dancing began, watching in real life what we had till now seen only in films. However, we soon left, and spent the rest of the evening playing table tennis. The other event was a freshers' day of introduction to college clubs and societies. Each of these had set up a stall or booth with volunteers explaining the scope of their activities and enrolling freshers.

I enrolled in the hockey and table tennis clubs as I had played these games in Kenya. There was a well-planned programme of matches for all the games, both on home grounds and for away matches. For the latter, we travelled by bus and returned in the evening. After every away match, tea and snacks were served to the visiting team. Matches were played on Wednesdays and Saturdays, with practice and coaching sessions on other afternoons. My first year at college, however, had to be devoted to serious study in order to qualify for admission to a degree course. I had to complete in one year what was normally a two-year course at the Intermediate Faculty of Science, University of London. This included laboratory work in the afternoons. At the end of the first year I did manage to pass my exams and opted for admission to a B.Sc. Honours course in geography, with geology as a subsidiary subject. There was also the choice between University of London and the newly chartered University of Hull. I chose Hull in order to be a part of a new venture in higher education, which was committed to serve those traditionally excluded from this opportunity.

During the first year, all the British students went home for Christmas holidays. For overseas students, family stays were arranged in villages around Hull. Atiq and I stayed with a pastor of the Congregationalist Church and his wife in

Wilby, a village in the low hills of Yorkshire Wolds. It was a week-long stay during which we participated in Christmas celebrations in the community. It was a white Christmas with snow covering the village and countryside, a very rural English setting. Our hosts were a kind, soft-spoken, middle-aged couple who ensured we were warm enough in this, our first winter in England. There was always a log fire in the drawing room. We were given hot water bottles at bedtime since there was neither central heating nor room heaters. We had long fireside conversations about our background and our religions. Atiq, as a devout Muslim, observed the discipline of offering *namaaz* five times a day. We walked through the village and into the fields, accompanying the pastor on his walks to meet members of his church's congregation. We were probably the first Asians to have stayed in this entirely English community. There was curiosity and Merry Christmas greetings were extended, but overall, a reserve prevailed. Our stay in the village was arranged by the local staff of the British Council in Hull. During the summer, the British Council also arranged a friendly cricket match for us, where a team comprising overseas students played against a country club near Hull. I played as a bowler and even took a couple of wickets with medium pace cutters on a wet pitch. As usual, there was gracious hospitality after the match.

Back at Camp Hall, even though it took some time and effort to make sense of their speech, I tried to converse with my English class fellows. Some of them became good enough friends to 'take the mickey out', tease me and make fun of my accent and use of language. I learnt to take it with good humour, which was appreciated.

One of these friends, Clive Higgins, a London boy, invited me to stay with his family in north London and arranged a summer job for me in a bakery in the vicinity. This was my first experience of a factory job. It involved lifting hot loaves from a conveyer belt and putting them on racks for wrapping and packing. On my first day, my work was near the ovens. I nearly passed out due to the intense heat and had to be shifted to a tank further away from the ovens. The work was entirely repetitive and utterly boring, even though there was 'music-while-you-work' broadcast in the background. One had to clock in on time to avoid pay deductions. There was a half-hour break for lunch and a couple of tea breaks. At the end of the week, the pay packet with crisp pound notes compensated for the drudgery to some extent. It also enabled me to indulge in watching films in a cinema hall and to see an Arsenal vs. Tottenham Hotspur derby football match at Arsenal's home stadium in Highbury. I became an Arsenal supporter, while my hosts were staunch Tottenham fans. They were a well-educated middle-class family. Staying with them, discussing politics and reading newspapers and books was a challenging experience intellectually. It broadened my horizons. I began thinking about how society and the state could be improved and even wrote some personal notes on this. Clive's older brother was a professional with enlightened views about independence for Britain's colonies and more equality amongst classes in Britain. However, he did not have any liking for football crowds and their craze about the game. He felt this was a distraction from the higher cultural and educational interests they were entitled to pursue as human beings.

After the holidays, I returned to Hull to begin the first year of intense engagement with life as a full-fledged student of the university. This involved academic work, sports, cultural pursuits, entertainment, students' union work, independent reading and informal discussions, close friendships, hostel life, digs, living in a flat, field trips and holiday travel.

In the very first year of studies, a whole range of new vistas in knowledge was opened up through different courses in geography and geology. There were courses in physical, human, historical, economic and regional geography, and palaeontology, stratigraphy, mineralogy, and crystallography in geology. With a lot of new terminology, considerable memorisation was involved, but the stress was always on understanding the connections, patterns, cause and effect, logical arguments, and experimentation. There were end of term and final year examinations as well as writing assignments on various topics, but no constant testing. The lecturers were specialists in their disciplines and devoted to encouraging its pursuit among the students, with special attention given to each student through tutoring. During field trips and laboratory work, there were opportunities for informal conversations and exchanging anecdotes.

During a practical session in palaeontology, the lecturer, Dr Penny, gave me some samples of fossils I had not seen before. He asked me to suggest a classification of these based on my observation of their features. When he saw the result of my effort, he was both pleased and surprised to see that what I had achieved was quite similar to the established scientific classification of this species. In a practical session in cartography, our class was asked to reproduce a scaled down version of a portion of a map on a larger scale. I produced a simple black and white sketch showing the main features of the locality. This too was admired by the lecturer and students. Experiences like these gave me a lot of confidence and happiness, and helped me to overcome the sense of inferiority inculcated over years of growing up in colonial regimes with entrenched white British supremacy.

Studies in subsidiary geology were completed in the first two years of the degree course. The third year was devoted solely to geography, with a specialisation in political geography with Professor King, an authority on the Balkans and the Middle East. He was a short, compact figure who smoked a pipe and wore a grey overcoat and a broad-brimmed hat. He had the accent and air of an Oxbridge don. There were only two of us enrolled in this course. We met Professor King in his room and listened to his lectures/anecdotes about the geopolitical changes that came about after World War I. He shared his books with us and gave us assignments on his research areas. One of the requirements for the course was research based on original sources of information. I was asked to find out about the changes in the manufacture of iron at a smelter in Middlesborough. For this, I spent a week in the city, pondering over the records of the enterprise for the production of various types of iron. Professor King was pleased with my findings as they confirmed his own hypothesis on this matter.

This specialisation gave me a good background to understand world affairs and international relations. Other courses in geography and geology also helped me later in life to make better sense of social, political and environmental problems in the world, and how to tackle these politically, socially and educationally.

During the Easter holidays in my second year, I travelled to Italy on a travel and maintenance grant awarded by the University for a study tour with another student who was studying economics. My main interest was in the art and architecture of cities in central Italy, especially those from the Renaissance period. For this, I made a study of Berenson's classic book on Italian Renaissance.

At the end of three years, graduate degrees were awarded in three divisions—first, second and third. The second division had two sub-categories, one and two. I passed my final Honours examination with above average marks and was eligible for the second division. Since I was on the margin between 2-1 and 2-2, I had to go through an interview. I did not do well in this and was adjudged fit for a 2-2 division. There were no first division awardees, and only one student received 2-1. Academically average but accomplished all-rounder was the verdict of my peers at the end of my four years at Hull. In extra-curricular areas I took active part in sports, entertainment, the film society, students' union responsibilities, youth hostelling and travel. In sports, I became the vice-captain of the first division hockey team and played for the University in inter-university games. I also played in the second division table tennis team and tried my hand at cricket and tennis. I was elected a member of the students' union executive committee. In that capacity, I was given the responsibility to chair the entertainment committee, which organised weekly ballroom dancing, as well as an annual ball in the town hall of the city of Hull. This was fairly demanding work, involving arranging the music band, decorating the hall, inviting guests, and ensuring the smooth conduct of events attended by hundreds of students.

I also joined the university air squadron to learn flying on a small aircraft called the Chipmonk. After a few lessons, I realised I did not have the aptitude for this, nor did I fit in the snobbish superior-to-others culture of the squadron. There was another elite group I was invited to join, 'The 25 Club'. Its membership was limited to 25, composed of senior students and younger faculty. It held gatherings once a term at an expensive restaurant, with the stated aim to promote the appreciation of good cuisine, good wine and good conversation. Being a member made you feel that you had been recognised as a cultured person in the college community. Apart from these organised activities, the senior students hosted house gatherings for special interests like listening to music, poetry readings and topical discussions. I hosted some of these in my flat in my last year at Hull. These were some of my best experiences as everyone contributed to the richness in some way.

During my four years at Hull, there were two memorable events. Queen Elizabeth II visited the University and one of her engagements was to meet the students. We lined up along the path leading to the students' union building and greeted her as she walked past. Among the students she chatted with was a Bengali girl from East Pakistan. I remember the intense look she gave me as she walked past me. It was a look of genuine, benign interest in one of her 'subjects' from the British Commonwealth.

Coming from Kenya, I knew about the Queen's special connection with that country. It was during a visit in 1952 to the Treetops, a lodge built amidst the thick equatorial forest at the foothills of Mount Kenya, overlooking a waterhole, that she learnt about the death of her father, King George VI, and became the Queen of the United Kingdom and the Commonwealth. Personally, I had mixed feelings about the royalty, especially the British Crown, having grown up during the freedom struggle in pre-independence India, followed by a stay of three years in independent India and four years in the colony Kenya, and subsequently studying in Britain itself. There was resentment against the Crown as the symbol of colonial power and oppression. But there was also a sense of gratitude and loyalty by virtue of being a British subject and being employed in the colonial civil service, on study leave with the British government's support for my scholarship.

The other memorable event was a debate at a special general body meeting of the students' union on the motion, 'This house condemns the British armed intervention in Egypt'. The provocation for this was the nationalisation of the Suez Canal by the President of Egypt, Gamal Abdul Nasser, in 1956. Both France and Britain opposed this move and decided to punish Egypt and regain control of the canal. The attempt failed due to Egyptian resistance and the canal was blocked by sinking vessels at its entrance. Britain's action was undertaken by the Conservative government, with Sir Anthony Eden as the Prime Minister. There was widespread opposition to the action, both in Britain and worldwide. Our students' union debated the matter at length, with strong voices in support of the motion, notable among whom were Roy Hattersley and Kevin McNamara, the president and secretary of the union, respectively. (Both of them were later elected as Labour Members of Parliament and held key posts within the political party.) I also spoke in support of the motion, expressing dismay that in this age of enlightened de-colonisation, Britain had decided to revive its imperial gunboat policy of coercion. The motion was passed with a large majority as the Union had a strong presence of working-class students with sympathies for the Labour Party. My intervention in the debate enhanced my standing amongst the student body and faculty, though some of the Asian students from East Africa felt that as a British colonial civil servant, I may have committed an indiscretion that could adversely affect my career. However, I had no regrets and felt gratified to have summoned the courage to take a principled stand and express myself publicly.

Apart from 30 or so weeks of academic work and extracurricular activities at the university, we had nearly four months of holidays in the year when we had to provide for ourselves. All the British students went home, but most of the overseas students could not afford the cost of travel. We used the vacations to work and earn some money. In my first year, I worked at a bakery. For the next two years, I worked as a waiter at a family-run restaurant in York. In the fourth year, I did night shifts at a frozen peas packing factory. Over two Christmas holidays I took up postal delivery work. The earnings from these jobs enabled me to travel and visit places of interest.

Over the second summer holiday, I cycled from Hull to London through Lincolnshire and East Anglia, staying at youth hostels as a member of the Youth Hostels Association. These were low-cost facilities run on self-help basis, with duties assigned to members on arrival. These included help with cooking and serving meals, tidying up dormitories, gardening and washing dishes. Evening meals were followed by singing and storytelling around the campfire. There were also lively discussions and conversations over meals where we shared our experiences. With some of the travellers, addresses were exchanged and some of them became fellow travellers for part of the journey. The memorable sights during the journey included the Gothic Lincoln Cathedral, made of golden sandstone, with its twin towers and large, circular stained-glass window above the altar, and Ely Cathedral with its grey slate roof and tall conical spire. I also came across farm workers and students working in the fields, picking strawberries, and roadside stalls selling these and other country produce. One of the distinctive features of the country was the hedges along the road marking field boundaries, some laden with berries. It was summertime, when the English countryside is at its most vibrant in all its greenery and freshness. During my journey, there were occasional showers but also spells of sunshine. For the most part, my route took me through the low-lying plains of eastern England. Only nearer London did the landscape change into undulating hills, north of the valley of the Thames River.

I reached London a week after I had left Hull, having traversed unfamiliar routes, guided by maps specially pre-pared for youth hostellers. Closer to London, the fields were replaced by housing estates and busy commercial roads. I passed through Welwyn Garden City, one of the first planned townships, with its tree-lined avenues and parks. Cycling through London was a nightmare with the traffic swirling all around. Somehow I managed to reach the Marble Arch and found a room to stay at the East Africa House, which had been my first place of stay upon my arrival from Kenya in 1953. As luck would have it, there I met Neves Pereira, the tall Goan candidate who had offered me reassurance after my interview in Nairobi. He had been selected in the same year and was studying mathematics and physics at Leicester University.

After a week of wandering through unfamiliar terrain among strangers, I was glad to see a familiar face. Neves took me under his wing and easily persuaded me to park my bicycle at East Africa House and accompany him on a trip to the Continent. We took the ferry across the English Channel and arrived at Ostende. We travelled through Belgium, France, Luxembourg, West Germany, Switzerland, and Italy by train, bus, hitchhiking and walking. Soon we realised the limits of our resources. We stayed at youth hostels and often survived on one meal a day, augmented with rolls of baked bread and cheese. Neves, having lived in Portuguese Goa and cosmopolitan Bombay, knew a lot about Europe's treasures of art and music. So we spent a lot of time visiting museums, art galleries and famous architectural and historical places. Walking around the cities and towns, we also saw sites of devastation caused by bombing during World War II. Europe was still recovering from this cataclysm. There were even beggars and children in tattered clothes asking for food in Germany. Litter was strewn across the streets. However, recovery and reconstruction were well underway, with generous support from the USA under the Marshall Plan and the security umbrella of the North Atlantic Treaty Alliance (NATO). Of course, the Cold War had also begun, and there were tensions along the border of divided East and West Germany, symbolised by the Berlin Wall.

However, we got no inkling of these developments during our travels. Being with Neves for these two weeks forged a bond of friendship, almost kinship, that would last throughout our lives. Neves became like an older brother, guiding and supporting me with his maturity and wise advice. We had our differences, even quarrels, usually around our positions about Portuguese Goa as a colony in independent India. I was intensely proud and defensive about my newly gained national identity as an Indian, in contrast to Neves' sense of superiority about his European, Catholic, and therefore more 'civilised' background. He'd often belittle and mock Indian 'manners' and 'untidiness'. Sometimes these arguments and altercations would become unbearable for me and I'd walk away. But Neves did much of this to tease me. He'd always come after me, calm me down and we would continue our journey together. Neves and I continued our close relationship through our years in Kenya, USA, Canada and India. Our travels took us through the cities and towns of Brughes, Brussels, Luxemburg, Paris, Dusseldorf, Stuttgart, Frankfurt, Reutlingen, Tubingen, Heidelberg, Ulm, Zurich, Geneva, Berne, Milan, Genoa. We left the continent at Calais, headed by boat for Dover and then took the train to London.

There I stayed for a few days, awaiting the arrival of my brother Prem who, like me, had won the Kenya Government Scholarship for higher studies in England. He too had to get the pre-degree qualification. For this he was admitted to the Polytechnic at Kingston-on-Thames in the southwest of London. Accommodation as a paying guest with a family was arranged for him in Surbiton. He stayed there for a year. Subsequently, he gained admission to a B.Sc. Honours course in geology at Kings College, University of London, where he spent three years. After helping him to settle in, I returned to Hull for the third year of my stay there.

After the first two years at Camp Hall, I shifted to 'digs' or paying guest accommodation in north Hull, close to the university. This was with a working-class family of first-generation Polish immigrants. Mr and Mrs Peske were middle-aged. Mr Peske worked in a metal factory and was a staunch member of the factory workers' union. He left home early, so we only met over supper in the evenings and over weekends. He'd talk non-stop about the injustices of the capitalists and the rights of workers. He did not like being contradicted, so I learnt to listen, politely nodding in a noncommittal manner. Mrs Peske was kind and caring. She fed us a wholesome breakfast with eggs, baked beans, porridge, bread and tea, as well as supper—sausages, potatoes, vegetables, bread. My bedroom was without a heater, so she provided me with a hot water bottle to keep me warm under the quilt.

Over the Christmas holidays, I took up, for the first time, a job as a postman, sorting and delivering mail door to door. It was part-time work that began in the late afternoon with the sorting of mail—mostly Christmas cards and packages—by locality, street name and house number, in racks with boxes for groups of numbers. Each of these was then tied with a string into packages and carefully arranged in a leather mail bag to be slung over the shoulder. After this, we'd set out on buses or bicycles to the localities assigned to each of us. There we walked from door to door, delivering greeting cards, gift packages and letters to eagerly awaiting recipients in homes lit up with Bethlehem stars, nativity scenes and decorations. It was often bitterly cold with snow and ice on the streets, but there was an overall warmth of spirit, with the unfailing refrain of 'Merry Christmas' at every human encounter on the street or at the doors. On one of these evenings, with patches of ice along the footpaths, I slithered from house to house with my unusually heavy bag of mail, feeling utterly miserable and cold. I knocked on one of the doors. An elderly man opened the door and saw my plight. He asked me to come in, sat me down in a chair and poured me a hard drink. I swallowed it in one go and felt revived. A warm glow of gratitude and goodwill filled my whole being as I savoured the spirit of Christmas with these strangers who were strangers no more. I took out the mail I thought was for this address and gave it to the kind man. As it turned out, the mail was for another address. I apologised. My gracious host and his wife smiled at me indulgently and assisted me with my mail bag on the way out, with greetings of 'Merry Christmas!' Ever since, the spirit of kindness and human warmth around this time of divine descent on Earth has abided with me and found expression in the exchange of Christmas greetings with friends near and far.

During the summer holidays of 1956, I worked as a waiter at Young's Hotel and Restaurant in York. The owners were a Jewish couple, Mr and Mrs Young. Mrs Young was the real boss at the reception, while Mr Young took care of behind-the-scenes tasks. The restaurant was located close to the imposing York Munster and the Shambles, a cobbled street in existence since medieval times, preserved in its old form as a tourist attraction with its small curios, antique shops and cafes. The restaurant was popular with tourists. Sometimes it served exotic dishes, including Indian curry, together with traditional English fare like roast meat with Yorkshire pudding and jacket potatoes. My job involved taking customers' orders and serving their meals in courses. I was the only non-English staff. Occasionally, customers who had served in India would engage me in conversation and share their memories. They'd always leave a generous tip.

Later that summer, Prem and I travelled through northern Europe, traversing Netherlands, Denmark, Norway and Sweden by train, bus and boat. Mostly we stayed in youth hostels. In Norway, we spent a couple of days with one of Prem's friends, whom he had met through scouting. His house was a neat wooden structure, set on a hillside in a forest. There we learnt about Norwegian goat cheese (*Yatust*) and smorgasbord, eaten with salad, salami sausages and fresh wild honey. The most awesome parts of the journey were the rides through the fjords of Western Norway, with long meandering bodies of seawater flanked by massive mountains. The spectacular might and majesty of that landscape induced both wonder and humility.

That same year I made a trip to Paris to spend the week of Easter holidays in the company of Monique, a nursing student I had befriended in Hull. She had jet black hair, sparkling eyes and always spoke with passionate exuberance in her highly French-accented English about the rich artistic and literary treasures of Paris. During my visit, Monique took me to the great art galleries and studios, explaining the nuances of the various styles, temperaments and lives of artists, especially those of the Impressionist school, like Toulouse-Lautrec, Chagall, Manet, Degas, Gauguin and Van Gogh. We walked the streets along the Seine, which was lined with pavement artists. Monique took me home to meet her family, who lived in a spacious suburban villa. I was warmly received by them and treated to a full-fledged seven-course French dinner. Each course consisted of a single item with the appropriate flavouring and trimming, cooked just before serving. There were long intervals between courses, filled with conversation about France, India, England—mostly in French, with Monique acting as interpreter. Before leaving Paris, I bought several booklets with paintings of Impressionists. Monique supplemented these with a few of her choice as gifts. Overall, the week was an enriching experience spent in the company of a native of Paris who loved, and was knowledgeable about, her beautiful city.

My last summer holidays were spent first on a job with a frozen pea-packing factory, followed by three weeks observing the teaching at a primary school near Hull (taken up later in this chapter), and ended with a 10-day hike in the Lake District of Cumberland.

The factory job involved picking up packets of frozen peas on an assembly line and putting them in cardboard boxes on moveable racks. The work was done during night shifts from 10.00 PM to 6.00 AM, with two 10-minute tea breaks and one half-hour break. The factory floor temperatures had to be kept low for the frozen peas, which were sent to cold storage after packing. This was my first such experience. One clocked in attendance on a machine and had to maintain a certain fixed tempo of work. We had an Irish supervisor who kept us under close watch, often shouting and reprimanding us for lapses and under-performance. No talking or communication was allowed amongst workers except during breaks.

To cope with the utter drudgery of the task, I tried to devise variations in movements and rhythms. On the first few days, one constantly watched the movement of the clock hands, but that only aggravated the feeling that time was not moving as fast as it should. After a while, one became better adjusted and stopped paying attention to the passage of time, starting to concentrate on the pace and quantity of work instead. One began to exceed targets, which evoked a sense of achievement. But the end of the shift at daybreak was always a moment of great relief and release. I would walk back to our digs with my friend, Anwar Sheikh from Nairobi. For the next couple of hours, we'd flop onto our beds and sleep. We would wake up for breakfast, usually eggs, baked beans or sausages, porridge or cornflakes, and sleep again till late afternoon. The factory was located in Cleethorpes, Northeast Lincolnshire, a small seaside holiday resort and fishing port with sandy and gravelly beaches below a cliff-lined coast. This is where we took walks in our free time. After three weeks of this spirit-breaking but remunerative routine labour I returned to Hull before undertaking my next assignment.

This entailed three weeks of observation in a village primary school near Hull—a requirement for the postgraduate diploma course in Education at Oxford, where I was to go next. Here I saw firsthand the progressive, child-centred play and activity methods that had been introduced in primary education in England through post-War reforms. It took me back to my teacher training experience in Mombasa under Miss Walker, who had brought this approach to East Africa. It was gratifying to see the importance given to primary education as the foundation of healthy growth and joyful learning for children. There were age-specific facilities, curricula and learning material. Well-cooked midday meals were provided under the supervision of neatly dressed female assistants. There were spacious classrooms, with wall displays of pictures, charts, maps and children's paintings. The key person was the class in-charge, who taught most subjects by integrating them through group work on projects. Apart from textbooks, every class had its own library. There were no exams at the lower primary level. The first exam was held at eleven plus (11+), after which they were divided into streams based on their 'intelligence quotient', which was determined through special tests. After completing three weeks of observation in the primary school, I packed and shipped my belongings while preparing for the move from Hull to Oxford.

Then I took off for a walking holiday in the Lake District, renowned for its beautiful landscapes and traditional villages, immortalised in the poetry of Wordsworth. Situated in the west of England, the region experiences frequent rains even during the summer. However, during the week I spent there, it stayed sunny, with clear blue skies. I walked from the railhead in the northeast, through the hills, dales, scars and fells of the mountainous core, to the railhead in the south. I stayed at youth hostels that provided bed, breakfast and supper at nominal charges. I took lots of photos with my small Canon camera and preserved these as slides. The Lake District, with its rich natural beauty and cultural heritage, had been designated as a national park and strict restraints were imposed on any activity that might spoil it. As a result, there were few motorable roads through the area, but plenty of well-marked paths and trails through the woods, pastures and barren rocklands. It was an uplifting experience, walking through the enchanting landscape that had fired the imagination of Romantic bards and artists who were appalled by the ugliness of the 'satanic mills' in industrialising England.

For me, this was a crowning and complementing of my knowledge of nature and man on Earth in aesthetic terms, which hitherto had been shaped by the purely scientific perspective underpinning geography studies at Hull. Of course, within me was a sense of the sacred intrinsic to

Nature, imbibed on pilgrimages to Haridwar on the banks of the river Ganga. But that had become dormant and overlaid by science, not to be revived for the seven years till I returned to India for a holiday and visited Haridwar in 1964. But more on that later. That sunbathed week in the Lake District immersed me in the inherent beauty of Nature, conserved by the English people's love for their countryside at the local level. This found expression in their gardens, hedges and fences, patches of wetlands and commons, parks, and all the way up to regions like the Lake District.

Looking back on my four years in Hull University six decades later, I am led to ask myself: What did it add up to? Did I make the most of this opportunity? Did I live up to the expectations and obligations attached to the scholarship granted to me as a civil servant in the department of education? If yes, to what extent? The short answer to this last question is 'yes', to a reasonable extent. To the first question, the answer is also 'yes' in overall terms, but 'no' in academic terms. Getting into the why and wherefore of this has to be saved for another time.

I had come to Hull from the backwaters of the British Empire as a shy, self-abnegating youngster lacking the ability to cope with the rigours of the academic regimen in a British university. There was also the mental conditioning, born from my colonial upbringing and setting, to see oneself as belonging to an inferior category of human beings. But there was something else too. There was, on the one hand, a resentment against the colonial order of hierarchy, with the urge to prove oneself on the terms and terrain of the rulers; on the other hand, there was also a deep sense of value and pride in one's identity as an Indian, with the shared heritage of an ancient civilisation and culture that had awakened to its own destiny and gained independence as a nation.

In the first three years, the dominant motivation and drive came from my urge to prove myself as capable of holding my own in studies, sports and social life in the university. In the last year, there was more attention paid to my Indian identity, not so much as an abstract concept, but more as a kind of angst of separation and yearning to re-connect. I experienced this acutely during an afternoon in 1957 when I went to see Satyajit Ray's *Pather Panchali* in a cinema hall in London. The film had earned acclaim at the Cannes Film Festival and had received rave reviews in *The Observer*, my favourite Sunday newspaper at the time. As I watched the scenes of two children running across the lush Bengal countryside, mystified by the distant sound of an approaching train, my whole being was transported to my own childhood in Fatehjung, Punjab, near Rawalpindi. My own train journeys, Beji, the daily routines and rituals of the household, all came alive. I sat through the film in tears, yearning to recover my Indian self, which had been severed by the traumas of Partition and migrations and had been submerged, if not denied, by my newly acquired Anglicised self. That experience also reawakened the dormant sense that my destiny, my tryst, my self-fulfillment had to be realised through life and work in India.

In a similar vein, watching a dance-drama depicting the story of the Taj Mahal, performed by Uday Shankar's troupe in a theatre the same year, allowed me to reconnect with the living aesthetics of India's classical tradition. Even though it was my final year, with important examinations to be prepared for, I searched for and read books on Indian philosophy and religion by Dr S. Radhakrishnan, the President of India, recognised by discerning intellectuals in the West as a modern example of Plato's philosopher-king.

This detour, or rather, a 'circular return' to my own past as my foundational self, was certainly a distraction from the task of preparing for my final examinations. It took its toll. As a result, my academic achievement remained at an average level in the exams as well as in the *viva voce*. This resurgence of the past into the present, of the Indian into the

British, of traditional into modern, would remain an abiding characteristic of my growth over the coming years, with all their tensions, adjustments and contradictions.

To return to the synoptic view of my four years in Hull, there were rich gleanings from conversations over tea and coffee breaks, over meals, during walks and while cycling to and from University to hostel. Academic field trips and travel to faraway locales during sports also provided the opportunity to gain a better understanding of fellow students. Some of these flowered into friendships that continued even after leaving Hull. Contact was maintained through the exchange of Christmas/New Year greetings with Enid Fowler (née Armitage), Crawford and Wendy Baines, Terry and Jean Smith. Professor Jay Appleton, who taught human geography, and his wife Iris took a personal interest in me and invited me home for tea. We stayed in touch, and many years later my wife and I stayed with them during our visit to Hull. Terry Smith became interested in our work in India. He and his wife Jean were to visit us later, and on their return they would go on to raise support for our work. Terry also arranged a special meeting for me to address the alumni, retired staff and friends of Hull University. This gave me an opportunity to express my gratitude to my alma mater, especially to my Guru (mentor), Professor Appleton.

Let me conclude this overview by listing the values, skills and attitudes I acquired during my student life in Hull: orderliness, punctuality, rational thinking, politeness and good manners, being fair and imbibing a sportsman's spirit, democracy and civic sense, friendliness, sense of responsibility, self-reliance, taste in food, dress, music, art, architecture, literature, films, sense of adventure, taking up challenges, exploring new avenues of work, relationships, ideas, ability to listen and to communicate meaningfully, sense of individual self/one's self with its possibilities, freedom of choice, a sense of right and wrong, true and false. However, it was not all virtuous. There was also a seamy side, essentially pertaining to my own shortcomings, inadequacies and lacks.

University life at Hull was organised around the premise of freedom with responsibility for students and faculty. It provided a range of opportunities for the all-round growth of one's self around the academic pursuit of one's choosing, in my case geography. This required the student to build up a highly self-disciplined regime, especially in the use of time, in work and recreation, in relationships. Most British students had been prepared for this in the course of their school education. I did not have the benefit of this preparation, intellectually, emotionally or socially. On the contrary, my upbringing and education had been highly unsettled, with dislocations, neglect and traumas, interspersed with periods of care and guidance. Thus, I lacked the basic self-discipline to shape my new life. So this had to be learnt in order to succeed academically and socially as a member of the university community. Fortunately, the set patterns/routines of meals, classes and extra-curricular activities enabled me to do this to a certain extent. The lapses lay in my making the optimum use of my own time outside these routines. Alongside all this, there was perhaps also some inner constraint, resistance, caution towards a thorough immersion into the knowledge/ thinking and culture/behaviour of Western modernity, as well as some deep-seated, nascent sense of duty to 'desh', felt as '*deshbhakti, deshprem, deshseva*'. The seeds of these had been sown through the *sanskar* and experience of childhood and adolescence in the late stage of the freedom struggle in pre-Partition India.

I reached Oxford in October, a few days before the start of the Christmas term. My first task was to find accommodation. Walking around Wellington Square, I came across a 'To Let' sign on the British Council office. I walked in and met the official in charge, Robert Frost, who had retired from colonial service in Kenya. He immediately took me under his care and offered me the room on the third floor, with bed and breakfast tariff on a very reasonable rate, which I accepted. There was one other lodger from Sri Lanka (formerly Ceylon) named Wickramsinghe, who was doing his doctoral studies. We usually met at the breakfast provided by the resident caretaker's family and argued over India's role in the subcontinent. Robert Frost also encouraged and helped me to matriculate (that is, become accepted/enrolled) in Worcester College at Oxford University, which had been his own college during his studies in Oxford. He wrote a note recommending my name and asked me to see the Bursar at the College. I was immediately accepted. A slip with the following Latin inscription was issued with Reg. No. 2757–57 to certify this:

> *Oxonle, termino Michaelis AD 1957*
> *Die v mensis Decembrie*
> *Quo die comparaitcoram me*
> *Chand Kishore Saint*
> *E Collegio Vigorniensi et admonitusest de observandisstatutis bajas Universitatis, et in Matriculam Universitatisrelatus est.*
>
> C. M. Brown
> Pro. Vice Chancellor

I have still not figured out its full meaning but at the time, I felt quite pleased to receive this proper status as a member of a College, although still a rank below that of undergraduate and postgraduate students. Membership required fulfilling obligations to attend dinners and tutorials.

The venue of my studies was the University Department of Education in a residential area, Norham Gardens. This was a 15-minute walk from Wellington Square, across the Broad Street, past Keble College and through the University playgrounds. There I attended lectures and tutorials. The lectures covered a wide range of topics in the field of education, including its aims and principles, psychological basis, practice, the educational system in England and Wales and its present status, history, the history of educational thought, education in other countries and in underdeveloped areas, visual and aural aids, and the teaching of history and geography. Supplementing these were prescribed textbooks, notably Plato's *Republic*, John Dewey's *Education and Democracy* and A. D. C. Peterson's *Educating Our Rulers*. Both lectures and readings were introductions to the topic, but were at quite a high level of abstraction, which I often found difficult to comprehend at first reading. There were no topic-specific tutorials that could provide opportunities to probe the concepts with teachers, so one was expected to work these out oneself, through library work on meanings, contexts and references. I did this, but with insufficient rigour, and as the exam results showed, I was able to reach an average level of achievement. However, I did achieve 'distinction quality' in the special essay on one of the topics. As with my studies in Hull, this showed that I had the capability to grasp complex ideas, but lacked its application across different fields.

The group tutorials with our tutor Harold Loukes and five or so other students in the course were, in educational terms, the most gratifying and thought-provoking experiences of my year at Oxford. Harold, a senior professor, had an amiable and relaxed manner with the students. A wisp of a smile and his puckish sense of humour always put us at ease when we met in his study overlooking the garden. He'd begin by fiddling with his pipe and asking us how we were faring in the course and in general. Then he'd pose a question or share a thought or suggest a problem for us to respond to and reflect upon. He'd call upon one of us to begin the discussion and then let the process, the flow of the argument and counter-argument take its course, all the time listening intently and occasionally interjecting other possible perspectives on the issue. He always made sure that no one, including himself, dominated the conversation, while encouraging the reticent to open up. He addressed me as 'Saint' and often pointedly asked me to put forward my point of view. For me, the tutorials proved to be the best opportunities to learn a dialogic approach in education, which I later developed as my own pedagogy. Towards the end of the year I came to know that Harold Loukes was a Friend, a member of the Religious Society of Friends, the Quakers. His educational method, with its openness and regard for other points of view in the pursuit of truth, apparently had much to do with this background.

After the course of studies, teaching practice and exams, I received a certificate from the University of Oxford Delegacy of the Institute of Education for satisfactory completion of the course requirements of professional training. Based on this, I received a letter from the director of the department, specifying that on the basis of the standard I had reached in the Diploma examination, 'had you been going to teach in this country (UK), you would have been recommended to the Ministry of Education for recognition as a Qualified Teacher, and that would have been your status'.

I have mentioned these documents to show how seriously the maintenance of professional standards was taken in the British education system, achieved through an intermeshing of training and certification.

In terms of extra-curricular activities, I only took part in hockey. I went to the trials for the University hockey team. I performed quite well in the first half, making successful forays up to the opposition's goal posts. Then, for some reason, instead of scoring I kept passing the ball to a team-mate. At the interval the captain of the University team pointed this out, but I lost the opportunity to be selected. This was just as well, since in this, my fifth year in England, I did not have the stamina for the kind of preparation required to participate at that level. However, I did play a few matches with the Worcester College team against other colleges. Besides playing hockey, I attended some debates organised by the Oxford Union, reputed as a training forum for future legislators and politicians. These were always of very high standard, occasionally with invited speakers from the Parliament and other public figures. I sometimes felt the urge to speak, but could never muster the courage. I was afraid of making a fool of myself.

The Easter term was devoted entirely to practice teaching. I was assigned to Abingdon School in Abingdon, a small town 7 miles north of Oxford. It was a full-day school run on the public school pattern, with morning classes, a collective lunch, and afternoon sports and other activities. I was attached to a section of Class Nine. The school day began with an assembly, which was addressed by the headmaster after the daily prayers and inspirational readings. It set the tone for the day and maintained a direct rapport between the headmaster, staff and students as a congregation. Most of my work involved assisting the class teacher in marking attendance, checking homework and helping students individually. There were also duties during lunch time and at the end of the day.

After a couple of weeks, I was asked to take up lessons in selected topics in geography, history and civics. I prepared for these with the guidance of the subject teacher. This involved reading and library work as well as preparing teaching aids like charts and pictorial illustrations. The teachers sat as observers during my lessons. Most of the teaching was routine and manageable, but sometimes there were difficulties, even embarrassment, with some of the smart teenagers ganging up to deliberately test and disturb a young trainee-teacher. One such incident took place when I was asked by the teacher of general knowledge to take a lesson on India. I began the lesson by providing a broad geographical and historical background of the region—its location, climate, physical features, its ancient, mediaeval and modern rulers, freedom movement and independence. As I spoke, some hands began to be raised for questions. 'Do Indians worship the cow?' 'What is the Indian rope trick?' 'Are there holy men who wander naked?' 'Are there Maharajas in India who ride on elephants?' I tried to respond to these, saying, 'Yes, these things do exist, but they are not the main features of life in India. India is a modern country with facilities like railways, electricity, elected government and factories. Rope tricks and such notions are imaginary fables.' Suddenly, one of the students, the class hero, asked, 'Why is India occupying Kashmir?' I was taken aback as I was not prepared for this. I tried my best to explain the circumstances of Partition and what had led to the situation in Kashmir. The student was not convinced and kept pouring out his hatred of India and all that was wrong in its actions towards Kashmir. Eventually, the teacher in charge had to step in and take over.

Later, I learnt from the teachers and my tutors that many of the children in Abingdon School came from conservative middle-class families with business backgrounds. They had still not reconciled to the loss of the Empire and carried a strong resentment against India, whose leaders had been in the forefront of the anti-colonial struggle. Further, this region was Oxfordshire, in the Midlands, where Blenheim Palace, the ancestral home of Sir Winston Churchill, was located, and which bore a strong imprint of his avowed imperial conviction. Subjectively, I carried within myself my own ambiguous feelings about being a civil servant in a British colony, Kenya, along with my intense pride in India's newly achieved independence and key role in the Non-Aligned Movement outside the Cold War Alliances. This made me rather touchy about any criticism of India. As it turned out, I survived the experience and came through with an above average assessment of practice teaching, as mentioned by my tutor.

In the evenings I spent some time watching the news, and cricket and football matches on the TV in the lounge. These spells often grew longer due to fatigue after the day's work and lack of fitness. Sometimes there were students from other British colonies who would drop in and watch TV. Once, while talking to a Somali student, I inadvertently made a gesture with my foot pointed towards him. He was deeply offended and angry, nearly ready to hit me. I realised my error and apologised. It took him some time to calm down. He then explained to me that in his culture, pointing a foot towards someone was considered the depth of boorishness and uncivilised behaviour. This experience was a salutary lesson for being sensitive to the norms of other cultures.

At Worcester College, I fulfilled the formal requirements by attending a few dinners in the dining hall and a couple of tutorials with Colonel Wilkinson in his study in one of the old cottages. Worcester College, like most other colleges in Oxford, had its own unique architectural history spanning centuries and its own locational character, adjacent to a natural wetland traversed by a stream. It was also reputed for its well-maintained gardens, an important tourist attraction in the summer. As an educational institution, the college began as Gloucester College, set up in 1285 by the Benedictine Abbey of St. Peter at Gloucester, to train monks. The mediaeval cottages were built during that time. It became the residence of the Bishop of Oxford in 1543; later, it was re-founded as Worcester College in 1714 through the benefaction of a Worcestershire Baronet, Sir Thomas Cooke. From 1720 to 1884, its main buildings and a chapel were constructed with mostly Renaissance-inspired Georgian architecture. More recently, new buildings—Frank Sainsbury, East Ruskin Lane—have been added. Once situated on the edge of the city of Oxford, it is now the only college near the centre of Oxford with its own grounds and award-winning gardens. It has the reputation of being 'the loveliest and friendliest' college in Oxford, and is considered 'a community of scholars who alongside their studies are involved in social events, charity work, drama, music, sports.' Sir Jonathan

Bate, former Provost of this college, is the author of *Romantic Ecology*, a book I accessed recently as bearing on my interest in the human–nature relationship.

Since I was not involved in course work with any faculty in the College and spent only one year in the university, I remained a stranger to its 'community', unlike my four years in Hull. The well-established hierarchy and the proverbial English reserve gave me little opportunity to strike up an individual friendship with anyone.

My last days in Oxford were spent packing and shipping my belongings under the shadow of this negativity. Some time before my departure, Robert Frost, the director of the British Council, advised me to become a lifetime member of Worcester College. I did so by paying £10 as a life membership fee. As was customary, this enabled alumni to get special consideration while getting their children admitted to the college, apart from receiving annual reports and invitations to alumni events. It was also a way for the College to maintain contact with its students and call on them for endowment and other support.

Robert Frost also invited me to tea with his family at his country home near Oxford. We sat in their spacious garden, which was in full summer bloom, under a paragola made of wrought iron, amidst garden furniture of the same material. Wrought iron work was a traditional craft of the pre-industrial era, lyrically admired by Victorian aesthetic philosophers like John Ruskin. The garden and the cottage were perhaps part of a large country estate in the broad undulating hills and plains of the Midlands. It was an idyllic English setting, greatly sought after by colonial civil servants for their retirement after their 'hellish' duties in sustaining the Empire for God and country.

Here memory fails. I have virtually no remembrance of those few weeks between leaving Oxford and arriving in Kenya. My brother Prem was in London, so I would certainly have met him and perhaps stayed with his host family. I may have gone to Hull to say a final goodbye to my teachers, the Registrar Mr Craig, and my friends. But, try as I may, I am unable to recall any of this. Perhaps, as I was coming to an inevitable end of that phase in my life, I had already begun to disconnect from being a student and a citizen in the United Kingdom and enjoying the freedom and opportunity it had provided. Perhaps it was necessary to make this break and give myself that space-time of oblivion— that detachment—before returning to my life as an Asian civil servant in the segregated, three-tiered pyramid system of the colony of Kenya, with its restricted freedoms, racially-defined citizenship and social restraints.

Prem tells me that he came to Oxford and we spent a couple of days visiting my college, seeing the sights and punting along the river. Beyond that there is still little I can recall: an important formative phase of my life had come to an end, but there was no closure. Resonances and returns would continue for years to come, the latest as these memoirs.

Before moving on, let me say a few words about the Bohannons, the family who hosted Prem. Prem met John Bohannon at a boy scouts camp for the Wood Badge, the highest grade of competence for leaders and trainers in the Boy Scouts Movement begun by Lord Baden-Powell. John invited him to take up residence in the family as Prem was looking to shift from his Surbiton lodging. This proved a God-send for Prem. The Bohannons accepted him as one of the family. I stayed with them during my visits to London. They were always gracious in their welcome and hospitality. Mrs Bohannon, as a mother and housewife, made special efforts to make Prem feel at home and gave him support as he pursued his studies. Their son Graham, affectionately called Zoot, was like a younger brother for Prem. Years later,

Mrs Bohannon came to visit our families in Kenya. This ended in a tragedy, but more on this when I reach that time in this narrative.

Amnesia, forgetting, blanking out part of my time in England continued during the flight from London to Nairobi as I prepared to reconnect with the life I had left behind and had been out of touch with for five years.

3
Kenya
1958–61

Back in Kenya in July 1958, my first memory is of a visit to the Ministry of Education in Nairobi to report my arrival and find out about my posting. I was told I would be assigned to teach in the newly opened Technical High School in Mombasa. As I was about to leave, the director of Asian Education, Mr Sykes-Thompson, saw me and called me to his office. My file was on his table. He suggested I take up a position as a teacher trainer at the Asian Teacher Training College for teachers in Nairobi. Without a moment's hesitation I declined the offer, saying that I had just completed my professional training and needed to gain some experience and find opportunities to apply and test the knowledge I had acquired. He appreciated this attitude and wished me well in my career ahead.

On reaching Mombasa, I had to find a place to stay. Having been away in England for five years, I had lost contact with everyone I had known. Father had been transferred from Mombasa after a students' strike at Allidina Visram High School. He was now in Kisumu, on the shores of Lake Victoria. After joining duty at Technical High School, I learnt that Neves Pereira had also returned to Mombasa and was the head of mathematics at the Goan High School. I contacted him. He immediately arranged for my stay in shared lodgings with young Goan teachers at his school. They all had Portuguese names and were Catholic. Later, Suresh Amonkar, a Hindu Brahmin, joined us. We had a common mess with a cook and took responsibility by turns to manage it. Only Goan dishes were prepared, with rice and fish for every meal.

At the time Goa was still under Portuguese rule, but an Indian nationalist movement was underway, with support from India. Most of the Goans in Kenya, being Catholic, preferred Portuguese rule. There were heated discussions amongst us about the developments in Goa and about the merits or otherwise of being Indian or Portuguese. The rest of them spoke to each other in Konkani. The arguments were particularly intense between Suresh Amonkar and Correa, D'Cruz and D'Souza. Sometimes they would revert to their local identities in Goa and their caste origins before conversion to Catholicism. At such times, they would find affinities and common peculiarities amongst themselves. There was much teasing and nostalgia about these. Even though I could not follow much of this, I enjoyed their bonhomie. They were in Kenya on short-term contracts and visas for work. Suresh Amonkar, who came from a well-educated family with strong Konkan cultural roots, stood well above the others in performance. His father had started the New Goa High School in the 1920s as part of a mission of education for the indigenous Konkan community. Suresh was slated to take over the reins of this venture and had been sent to Kenya to gain some experience in a different setting. With the support and encouragement of the Principal, Mr Alphonso, and Neves Pereira, he introduced new dimensions in the teaching of English literature by directing a student production of the Greek play *Antigone*. This was a first of its kind event in Mombasa and earned applause across communities. Suresh returned to Goa after a year or so and we lost touch with each other. Decades later, in the 2000s, we would discover each other again, this time with our families and new generations, and a whole new dimension would be added to our lives in our 70s and 80s.

At Technical High School I was assigned to teach in the 'Modern' stream for the supposedly less intellectually well-endowed children. This was along the pattern of the three-fold streaming of secondary school education—Grammar, Technical and Modern—in the UK. The Grammar stream was for those with academic aptitude, the Technical stream for those with aptitude for technical skills and the Modern stream for those without aptitude for either, but with entitlement to basic literacy, numeracy and general knowledge. There were different textbooks for each stream. I had to teach geography, English and general knowledge. There were British and Asian teachers; British teachers taught English, technical subjects like metal craft, woodwork/carpentry and civil engineering as preparation for careers in engineering. Asian teachers taught mathematics, history, Gujarati and Urdu, physics and chemistry. The principal was a Goan, Mr Lobo.

My Asian colleagues were surprised that, despite my high qualifications, perhaps the highest among Asian teachers in the country, I was asked to teach the classes of 'mediocre' students. They attributed it to the prejudice of the principal against non-Goan Asians. Others thought it was due to the stigma attached to 'Saints', resulting from my father's transfer as punishment for the students' strike at Allidina Visram High School. Apparently, at that time the students of the Technical High School had joined in and had gone around shutting down classes, even indulging in a spot of vandalism by breaking windows in the nearby primary school. Years later, I learnt from Yunus Bagha, my student in Standard One in Mbheni Primary School, that the striking students had come there on cycle, but were thrashed and chased away by Mr Bhag Singh, the elderly Sikh assistant headmaster at the school in my time.

In these circumstances, I took the assignment as a challenge and felt it was my duty to educate the children placed in my care as best I could. The facilities were minimal.

Classes were held in an old primary school building that lacked fans. There were blackboards and white chalk as aids and separate textbooks. For geography, there was also a series called 'Real Geography', with case studies of actual settlements and activities at the local level in different regions: for instance, a dairy farm in Denmark, a sheep farm in New Zealand. There were black and white photographs, location and site maps, and text in simple English. I supplemented these with audio-visual aids like charts, country maps and coloured chalk. Using the photographs, I guided the children to make models on school grounds using soil, stones, leaves and twigs, cardboard cutouts, etc., with labels for names. Sometimes the principal, Mr Lobo, came to observe my teaching and showed his appreciation of my effort to instil confidence amongst the students.

This phase of my work at Technical High School lasted till the end of 1959. Mr Lobo retired and Mr Verghese, a Syrian Christian with Brahmin ancestry, was appointed in his place. He showed a greater interest in my background and education. He assigned me to teach senior classes in the Technical section, made me responsible for preparing the yearly timetable and consulted me about making improvements in the educational standards of the school.

Teaching geography to senior classes in the Technical School section gave me an opportunity to bring in more advanced knowledge of the subject. While teaching about the planetary system and movements around the sun, I used improvised dynamic modelling, with a light in the centre acting as the sun and a rotating globe moving around it to show the cycle of day and night and the seasons. Similarly, to explain the contours on a topographical map, I used a trough with a mound in the middle, gradually filling it with water and marking the increasing height as contours around the mound. A contour map would be a view of the lines seen from above. Decades later, this was recounted by Ramzanali

(Ramu) 'Parvana', my student from that class, now living in Canada. He came to see us in November 2015, travelling 17 hours by bus from Bhavnagar in Gujarat to Udaipur. He had come there as a volunteer teacher to work in a private school.

In one of the weekly school assemblies, I was asked to address the students and teachers. I dwelt at some length on responsibility and the need for teachers to set an example through their behaviour. I also spoke about the contrast in this respect between schools in the UK and those in Kenya. This was not liked by some of the teachers, who accused me of belittling the Asian staff in the presence of the British staff members. As expected, the latter showed appreciation for my outspokenness. This made me wonder whether I had done the right thing.

Another memorable incident involved pomp and ceremony. Towards the end of the year I was asked to organise the annual prize-giving day. The principal wanted it to be a big show. He was rather a vain person. He had studied for a Master of Education degree at the University of Birmingham and was perhaps the most qualified person in Asian education in Kenya. He specifically asked me to find a recording of music suited to his entry in the assembly hall at the head of a procession of the school's staff at the start of the function. Looking through my collection of LP records, I came upon Beethoven's Fifth Symphony, also known as the 'Emperor Symphony'. I selected the famous March within this symphony as the piece to be played. I had to take my own music system to the school to play it. On the day of the function, Mr Verghese appeared in his cream-coloured suit with his gown and tasseled cap. Hiding a limp in his left leg, he strode up the aisle at the head of the procession of staff members, who were dressed in simple shirts and trousers. All the students and guests stood up. The music was played on cue and concluded when Mr Verghese and the staff were seated on the stage. The rest of the function went off as planned. The irony and incongruity of it all was only revealed years later, when I discovered that the March in fact depicted Napoleon's retreat after his defeat in Russia. But such are the ways of human vanity that what mattered on that occasion was the pomp and blare of the trumpets and the beat of drums. Mr Verghese was pleased with my efforts to make the function a success. After this, I became his confidant. He'd call me to his office and discuss ideas for the school.

Outside school hours, I became involved in several activities. With the support of Mr Lawry, director of the local office of the British Council, I set up the Kenya Youth Hostels Association (KYHA). We identified institutions that could provide accommodation and food to young people at nominal charges during their travels. We organised adventure trips to local places of interest, like the limestone caves in the raised coral reefs along the coast, and to inland hills. A longer trip was organised to the Rift Valley in the Kenyan highlands to see the Great Escarpment and Lakes Naivasha and Nakuru, which are teeming with flamingos and other birds. Walking along the Escarpment, we ran into a group of Mau Mau fugitives. They were quite unconcerned about our presence. We considered it prudent not to engage in conversation about our venture and continued with our trekking. On our way back, in Nairobi, I met my friend Anwar Sheikh, a fellow student at Hull University, and persuaded him to take responsibility for the KYHA in Nairobi. He readily agreed and arranged a centre at Duke of Gloucester High School, where he taught history.

We also formed the Mombasa Film Society that screened artistic films by great directors like Federico Fellini, Louise Malle and Ingmar Bergman. These became popular with discerning British, African and Asian viewers. Little Theatre, hitherto open to Europeans only, permitted the screenings in its auditorium. This marked the beginning of social and cultural intermingling across racial boundaries.

These initiatives were carryovers from my interests in England. But there were other activities that emerged from new contacts to Mombasa as bearers of Indian folk and theatre traditions.

A Bhangra group was formed under the tutelage of Harbhajan Singh Preet, a talented stage actor and dancer recently arrived from Punjab. Ten of us got together and arranged a *dholak* (drum) player to play the bhangra beat. Practice sessions were held in the sports pavilion of a Catholic school for African children. Mr Preet demonstrated the basic steps, postures and arm movements. It was fascinating to watch the suppleness of his movements, despite his heavy build. After several weeks of hard work, we reached a level good enough for a public performance. So the Regal Cinema auditorium was booked. Silk kurtas, embroidered jackets and lungis were stitched. Turbans were made and stiffened with starch. We were encouraged to grow beards and moustaches. Invitations were printed and sent to Asian schools, clubs, societies and dignitaries of the town. On the night of the performance, it was a full house. This was the first time bhangra was being performed in town. We were terribly nervous but Mr Preet kept up our spirits. The performance was a great hit, even though we missed a step or two. For Punjabis in the audience, it was a moment of nostalgia for the life they had left behind.

Another venture was the performance of *Sacrifice*, a play by Rabindranath Tagore. This too was initiated and directed by Mr Preet. The play is about a priest from whom the goddess demands a human sacrifice to end a calamity that has befallen the country. The priest asks his disciple to sacrifice his beloved Aparna. The disciple argues and agonises with the priest, who remains adamant. In the end, the disciple sacrifices himself. I played the role of the disciple. Aparna was played by a Goan girl as no Punjabi or Gujarati family would permit their daughter to perform in public. The priest's role was played by Mr Preet with great professional aplomb. The performance was a huge success.

Apart from these special events, there were informal gatherings at Dr Suryakant Gor's home. I had shifted there and lived in a two-room flat on the top floor. On Saturday evenings we played cards and listened to Indian classical music late into the night. Sometimes there were heated discussions about how India was faring after independence. There was also a lunch visit by a prominent trade union leader and politician from Gujarat, Dr Indulal Yagnik. He was dressed in immaculate white khadi. I could not follow much of the talk in Gujarati, but was quite impressed by his calm, collected demeanour. Later, I came to know that he was a key figure in the movement for statehood for Gujarat.

I took up membership of the British Council library. There I came across the book *A Saint on the March* by Hallam Tennyson, which I borrowed and read without a break. The book was an account of the three months the author had spent with Vinoba Bhave, Mahatma Gandhi's spiritual heir, in 1959 during his Bhoodan–Gramdaan Padyatra (gifting land, gifting villages walking campaign). This was his inspired, non-violent response to the Communist-led armed peasant uprising for land redistribution in Telangana in south India. According to the author, Vinoba had evoked a new spirit of sharing land with landless tillers and cooperation for self-reliant village upliftment, with support from thousands of dedicated workers engaged in identifying surplus land, completing formalities for its transfer and spreading the Gandhian message of 'Sarvodaya'—awakening of all, for the good of all. This touched some hidden seed of dreams and ideals in my subconscious, planted during India's independence movement, imbuing it with an inner urge to be part of a movement for their realisation. After that, I could not sleep for three nights, with the refrain 'I should be there', 'I should be there' ringing in my head. I went to work in a daze. But faced with the reality of an obligation to serve for at least three years after studying on scholarship, the storm subsided. Nonetheless, it left a mark, a reminder of some hidden tryst with Gandhi and destiny in and for the land of my birth.

During longer holidays I travelled to Kisumu, a port town on Lake Victoria, where Father had been posted in Kisumu High School. There I met his colleagues and the families he had befriended. In the evenings, we walked along the lake shore. Our conversation was never easy. He certainly felt pride in having an England-returned son and, as a father, he was concerned about my getting married and settled in life. I was a highly eligible bachelor in the community. On one occasion, I asked him for financial help to buy a car befitting my status as a Class 1 Education Officer on par with Europeans. He didn't refuse, but his silence was eloquent. I had to be self-reliant in these matters.

Outside school there were fewer involvements in the months that followed. I mostly kept to myself, other than regularly attending the weekly Havan and prayers at the Arya Samaj on Sundays. This reformist Hindu movement had played an important role in shaping our family. Father, who had since retired and come to stay with me, was regularly invited to give talks at their functions. Soon after my return from England, he took me along on one occasion. I was welcomed by the organisers and invited to say a few words. Hesitantly I went to the stage. Facing the audience, I began talking about bringing in new ideas and giving young people responsibility in the organisation. I spoke in Hindi with surprising facility. There was appreciation and applause. After I sat down, Father took the stage. He all but condemned what I had said, terming them new-fangled ideas that were not suited to Indian traditions. That defused any desire I might have had to be of service to the community.

After that, for over a year I kept a distance. Eventually, however, grappling with an inner void and vulnerability, I felt the need for some spiritual solace in a collective setting. I had memories of early morning and evening prayers, chanting Vedic mantras, during my year at the Arya Samaj Gurukul Rawal, the site of present-day Islamabad in Pakistan. Arya Samaj in Mombasa had a competent priest with knowledge of rituals and the ability to explain their significance. I found sitting through the ritual and chanting in unison a calming experience.

But unbeknownst to me, something more profane was afoot in those sacred hours. One day I noticed one of the ladies in the congregation staring hard at me. I ignored it, but every time I looked up, there were those dark eyes with an intense look. After Havan, while distributing *prasad*, she would give me a kind look and a large helping of the offering. It was only later that I learnt that she had three daughters of marriageable age. She was playing her part in making me amenable. In Punjabi, there is an idiom to describe this: *dore dalna*, literally, casting a web.

A few months after my return, I had enough savings for a car. I purchased a secondhand Fiat 1100 in excellent condition and started driving to work. On the way, I'd give a lift to people I knew. Among them were two young ladies. Both had been my students at Mbheni Primary School and were now working as trained teachers. It seemed both were interested in me as an eligible bachelor. During the ride we talked about our work and their career ambitions. I did not find either of them particularly attractive. There was also the unwritten code of sanctity of the teacher–student relationship, which is not to be violated by any unbecoming behaviour. Despite this, the grapevine spread the impression that I was considering marrying one of them, with their mothers working in their own ways to enhance their prospects. One of the families was more proactive—the girl's mother was the very same lady whom I had noticed staring at me during Havan. They invited me home for a meal. The mother wanted a quick decision, promising me a gift of an expensive wristwatch at the engagement. This was highly embarrassing. I refused to make any commitment, saying I had to consult father. The matter was again raised when Father visited Mombasa. He too refused their proposal for a formal engagement. Meanwhile, the daughter had been selected for a short course of training in England. Prem told me she stayed with his hosts, the Bohannons. On her return, she boldly told me that I should not feel any obligation towards her. Thus ended this episode of 'near engagement'!

In the holidays of December 1960, Prem, who had returned from England and joined Kisumu High School, persuaded me to make a tour of Uganda in my car with him and two other friends. I drove from Mombasa to Kisumu. From Kisumu, along with Prem and another friend, we went to Jinja, where we picked up Dharamvir Shaunak. We stayed for a night with his family. This was next door to the Sharmas, who, as fate would decree, were to become my in-laws three years later. From there we headed west, along a road mostly running parallel to the equator but crossing it at some points, where we encountered signboards proclaiming, 'You are now crossing the Equator'. We passed through the lush green countryside, with thatched mud huts amidst farms with plantains, jackfruit, palm trees and patches of maize and cassava. Our destination was the Kilembe copper mines near Kasese, where an erstwhile colleague, Kamla Dani, had moved to be with her husband, a mining engineer. He took us into the mine and showed us ore veins and ways of extracting the ore. The workers inside the mine were all Africans, with a few Asian supervisors employed by Kilembe Mines Limited, a Canadian company.

After enjoying our hosts' warm hospitality for two days, we set off towards the Uganda–Congo border. The road ran along the northern side of Ruwenzori Mountains. It had a single motorable track that allowed one-way traffic at fixed hours. I drove all the way, reaching the border after three hours and descending into the thick equatorial forest of eastern Congo. We were allowed to cross over into Belgian territory, where there was an encampment of pygmies. We then drove back to the border post in Uganda.

On the return journey, I took the wheel despite being tired, negotiating the tortuous road till we reached Fort Portal by nightfall. It was late and we did not have a place to stay. So we decided to drive on northwards to Toro Game Reserve. Dharamvir Shaunak took over the driving. I sat in the front seat, with Prem and another friend in the back. Since we were all tired, we sang for a while to keep awake. An hour or so into the journey, all of us, including Dharamvir, must have dozed off. We were woken by a crash. The front of the car had hit a rock and it had turned turtle. Miraculously, the three of them were unhurt. They extricated themselves from the car and pulled me out. My head had smashed into the windscreen, which had lacerated the left side of my face. We sat benumbed on the roadside in the pitch dark. After a short while, a delivery van with Asian traders arrived from the north. They helped us turn the wrecked vehicle over and moved it away from the track. Then they took us all to Fort Portal and got me admitted to the main hospital. There, another miracle awaited me. A young American doctor who had specialised in plastic surgery was working there as a Peace Corps volunteer. He immediately carried out the procedures to rotate and stitch the skin hanging loose on my left cheek and forehead. The skin on the left eyelid had also been cut and had to be stitched, but the eye was not damaged. This timely attention by a competent professional saved me from having a permanent, ugly scar on my face, or worse. For this I shall always be grateful. After a few days of treatment and attending to the formalities related to our car accident, we returned to our homes.

Back in Mombasa, I rejoined my duties at school, my face and eye still patched for protection. As the news spread, there was some sympathy, but overall people kept their distance and interest in my eligible bachelorhood declined. This was a relief. Breaking the half engagement with Vijay Kundi had led to a virtual social boycott against me by the Hindu Punjabi community. Once, while leaving a neighbourhood shop, I had to face the wrath of her father who threw some choice Punjabi abuses at me, forcing me to beat a hasty retreat. Apart from work, I kept to myself, reading and listening to music.

I also remembered that in the course of our conversations, the principal, Mr Verghese, had encouraged me to pursue a Masters degree in education at the University of Birmingham. I decided to follow his advice, applied and was accepted for the course. My overseas home leave was due later in the year. This entitled me to three months' salary and passage to and from England. The course required four terms at the University. I applied to the Ministry of Education for permission for further studies and extended leave. I was granted a year's unpaid leave of absence. After fulfilling my duties at school, I left for England in September 1961.

Kenya became independent in December 1963. Before that, it had been a segregated society, so there was no mixing or socialising amongst Asians, Africans and Europeans. In 1963, I opted to work in an African teacher training college in Kenya's highlands. I maintained good relations with my students, the African staff and the principal, who was also African. This dynamic continued in the Coastal Teacher Training College at Shanzu, which had a multiracial staff with a British principal. On my departure, four years later, one of the African students wrote with admiration about my relationship and approach to teaching, and regretted my leaving.

I remained in desegregating Kenya only for four years, from 1964–68. I, with a Punjabi Sanatan Dharmi and Arya Samaj background, married in 1963 in the traditional manner. I left for the USA in late 1968 and spent three-and-a-half years there before returning to India for good, which I had always wanted to do.

4

England / Kenya

1961–62 / 1963–64

On reaching Birmingham, I was able to find paying guest accommodation with Geoffrey and Eva Ostergaard. Geoffrey was a professor of political sociology at the University of Birmingham. Living with the Ostergaards was in itself a learning experience. Geoffrey had taken part in the Spanish Civil War against the dictator General Franco. He was an anarcho-pacifist who had made a deep study of anarchist and socialist thought and movements. He was involved in the peace movement and was associated with anarcho-pacifist thinking, with its underlying principles opposing the use of violence for social change, as well as the Campaign for Nuclear Disarmament. Later, he studied the Gandhian movement and non-violence and published *The Gentle Anarchists* (1971) and *Non-violent Revolution in India* (1985). Over supper, he'd try to engage me in conversation on these areas, of which I had very little knowledge. He was understanding and encouraged me to learn more. Eva was an excellent cook. She also gave piano lessons to students.

For the M. Ed. degree I opted for courses in educational philosophy, educational psychology and statistics. The department had a top-class faculty and research facilities. Like me, most of the students were experienced teachers with whom one could engage in serious conversation about topics in our curriculum. As in Oxford, there were tutorials in small groups, with regular writing assignments and extensive readings. In addition, there were common lectures by senior professors.

They introduced us to the theoretical aspects of education. Professor M. V. C. Jeffreys, author of *Mystery of Man* (1957), brought in the ideas of Martin Buber, Emmanuel Mounier and Teilhard de Chardin. Professor E. A. Peel was an expert on Jean Piaget, a Swiss psychologist doing path-breaking work on the sensory-motor, cognitive and emotional growth of children. E. Hallworth taught us about the learning theories of Pavlov and other behavioural psychologists. Carr was a specialist in research methods like intelligence tests, sociometry and attitude assessment. Ruth Beard introduced us to basic concepts and techniques in statistics, including the use of computing devices like slide rule and Kurta, precursors to personal computers and laptops. A. H. Halsey taught us about group behaviour and social relationships in classroom situations. There was a strong emphasis on the emerging science of communications, verbal and non-verbal. We were also introduced to concepts such as gestalt, the 'I-Thou' relationship, dialogue, the Divine Milieu and Maslow's hierarchy of needs, as well as their application in educational practice. Jean Piaget's work gave me leads for further research for a possible PhD on cognitive development in non-Western children.

Twice a month there were extramural public lectures by eminent speakers, with opportunities for the audience to pose questions. In a lecture on the scientific method, the speaker contended that normally, a word written on a blackboard with a piece of chalk would be read for its meaning. However, it could also be seen as an assemblage of particles of chalk. It'd be quite scientific to count the number of chalk particles. This intrigued me. I asked, 'What purpose would that serve?' He replied, 'It may not serve any purpose, but it'd be a scientific pursuit.' I was not convinced. Later, some of my friends admired my courage, or mocked my foolhardiness.

Besides coursework, I played hockey for the University a few times. However, the better part of my spare time was spent with a few friends from India. They were a sizeable group doing postgraduate research, mostly in engineering subjects, for which Birmingham University had special expertise. The exception was U. R. Ananthamurthy, who was doing his doctoral studies in literature in the Department of English, which was headed by Richard Hoggart. I developed a special friendship with Chandrashekhar Sastry (Chandra). He was only a few months older than me, but had greater composure and maturity. He was a great listener with a wide range of interests.

We met over lunch breaks with other students from India. They'd discuss the political situation there under Nehru, often critically. I'd listen intently. Over the weekends, there were gatherings at the homes of some of the Indian students with their families. Traditional Indian meals were prepared. This was where I was introduced to south Indian cuisines. On one occasion, a night-long Kathakali performance was organised with a visiting group of artists from Kerala. They enacted the story of Nala–Damayanti. I watched it for the full five hours, utterly enchanted by the intricate gestures and rhythms, even though I could not follow the language.

Over the summer vacation, Chandra and I went to Ireland. We hiked in the Wicklow Mountains south of Dublin for a week, staying in youth hostels. It rained most of the time, but everyone we met on our way greeted us with 'Nice Day!'. Wholesome meals with soup, homemade bread and cheese warmed us up on our arrival in the hostels. Chandra also got me involved in an inter-university debating competition for Indian students. Dr Ghosh and I represented Birmingham University. The final was held in London. We were the winners for that year.

After three terms of coursework and exams, in the last term I had to carry out original research for my dissertation. I focused on studying the intellectual abilities of Punjabi immigrant children in schools in Smethwick, an industrial town near Birmingham. The children had come with their illiterate parents from the Doaba region in Punjab to a post-war Britain that was dependent on labour from erstwhile colonies in Asia, Africa and the Caribbean. Their fathers worked in smelting foundries. They lived in congested homes, often sharing rooms in day/night shifts. The children had no facility with English. With regard to their intelligence, my research hypothesis was that it should have a normal pattern of distribution. To test this, I used a non-verbal intelligence test. Being a Punjabi, I could explain the test in their language and also elicit information about their background. I visited some of the families and saw their living conditions. Despite the hardship, they were warm in their hospitality, even offering me a meal of *sarson da saag* and *makki di roti* (mustard leaves hash with maize bread). The test results showed that my hypothesis was valid.

Prem returned from England in mid-1960 and joined Kisumu High School to teach geography. Father was already there. Prem got married in December 1961. This was self-arranged. I could not attend the marriage as I was in England. His wife, Raksha, belonged to a family who lived in Nairobi. She had studied in the Sanatan Dharma Girls School, though the family was Arya Samaji. She had also become a trained teacher. Their son, Sanjay, was born in November 1962.

Father took early retirement in 1963, by which time I had returned, and moved to Mombasa to stay with me. He was concerned about getting me married. He asked a friend, Mr Bector, to advise me on this. Mr Bector was a soft-spoken, bald, middle-aged man. He was a master at persuading young men at a 'loose end'. Softened and sobered by the experience of two breakups, I let him take the initiative to find a match. Through him, the Sharma family in Jinja (with whose neighbours, the Shaunaks, we had earlier stayed on the first leg of our Uganda safari) sent a proposal for their younger daughter, Sudesh. A meeting was arranged at a mutual friend's house in Nairobi. Both our families, Mr Bector, as well as our hosts, the Behls, were there. Prem and Raksha were also there. I had been away on a youth hostelling trip to Rift Valley and reached Nairobi just in time for this get-together. I decided not to dress formally and joined the gathering in my dusty, casual clothes. Sudesh was also simply dressed without any makeup. We saw each other, but no words passed between us. Prem was dressed for the occasion and was his usual ebullient self. There were refreshments. Pleasantries were exchanged and the meeting came to an end. Later, Sudesh told me that she had thought Prem was the eligible young man she was supposed to see. This was amply understandable, given the nature of the occasion.

Back in Mombasa, I continued with my routine and gave no further thought to this possibility. A few months later, I received a letter from Prem, telling me that Sudesh was planning to visit Kisumu to attend a wedding in a friend's family. He suggested that I should come to Kisumu, which would give me a chance to meet Sudesh on my own. I was not certain and wrote back asking Prem whether this was the right time to meet, to which he responded in the affirmative. I drove to Kisumu in the secondhand Volkswagen Beetle I had bought recently. There, I asked Sudesh to join me for a drive. We drove to the top of a hill overlooking Lake Victoria and shared our thoughts. Finally, I told her that eventually, I planned to live in India. I asked her whether she would be prepared for that. She said 'Yes'. That was reassuring for me. I told her that as far as I was concerned, we could go ahead with the marriage.

Subsequently, through correspondence between families, arrangements were made for us to be married on 21 December 1963 in Jinja. Since there was no woman in our family in Mombasa, Father and I had to make all preparations ourselves. My in-laws asked me to get a gold ring and a wedding suit made as a gift on their behalf. For this, I went to Nairobi and took the help of Prem's sister-in-law, Sheila. Invitations were also sent to friends in Kenya and family in India.

Closer to the date of marriage, I drove with Father to Nairobi. We were joined there by Bharati Trikha, the wife of a distant cousin, Dr Shyamlal Trikha, on my mother's side in Kenya. We left Nairobi early in the morning, reaching Jinja in the afternoon. Arrangements had been made for our small marriage party to stay in a school hall. A Mercedes car belonging to Inder Singh Gill's family was decorated for the bridegroom to be driven to the Sharmas' home, where the marriage ceremony was to take place. Pandit Dixit, a Sanskrit scholar, had been requested to conduct the ceremony. On my arrival there, we were received by my in-laws, with solemn garlanding and embracing by peers. I was asked to sit under the *mandap*. The bride was then brought in and seated next to me. Pandit Dixit then took charge and led us through the rituals while chanting *mantra*s appropriate to each part. He would pause and explain the significance of each ritual in English. The concluding and most important ritual was the seven perambulations around the sacred fire, accompanied by vows and obligations for this lifelong bond. I followed the whole procedure with interest and alertness. After the ceremony and dinner for the guests, our party returned to the school hall for the night. During dinner, someone recited the Sehra, an elegy in praise of the bride and bridegroom, composed for the occasion by Mr Bector.

The next morning, we returned to the Sharmas' for the bride's departure, always a poignant moment for the family. On our way back, Sudesh and I sat in the rear, with my father in front and Bharati driving. Halfway through the journey, something went wrong with the car—it would not pick up speed. We managed to reach Nairobi fifteen hours after leaving Jinja. Later, it was found that one of the plugs in the engine had come unstuck. The car had been running on only three cylinders. The morning after that, Sudesh and I left for our honeymoon at a hotel on the slopes of Mount Kilimanjaro in Tanganyika. It was an old-fashioned German colonial resort with separate chalets for honeymooning couples. It provided excellent, wholesome Western meals, with the luxury of breakfast served in one's room. We spent a week in that enchanting setting, with heavenly views of the snow of Kilimanjaro and walks in spacious, well-maintained gardens.

Father had returned to Mombasa. We joined him there for a few days. After independence, the education system in Kenya was being integrated. I learnt of an opportunity to teach in a hitherto African teacher training college, Kagumo College, in Nyeri at the foothills of Mount Kenya, situated at a height of 5,500 feet above sea level. I applied to teach there and was accepted. We requested Father to live with us, but he dreaded the cold weather that had made life so difficult for him in Eldoret, which was at equivalent altitude. He decided to stay in Mombasa on his own. I felt guilty about this, but a choice had to be made.

We reached Nyeri in early January 1964. I reported to the principal, Mr Popkin, and was assigned duties. To begin with, we were lodged in a second-grade house for clerical staff. This reflected the old hierarchical mindset of the principal. Later, when he realised that my appointment was as Education Officer, he shifted us to a teaching staff bungalow. Most of the teaching staff was British, but a few Americans and Canadians had arrived under the Peace Corps Programme. A couple of African faculty had also joined. The only other Asian staff member was a physical education instructor, Roshan Lal, from Machakos. With a Master of Education degree and Postgraduate Diploma in Education, professionally I was the most highly-qualified among the staff. I was asked to take courses in teaching methods, educational psychology and approaches to education. All the students were African, mostly from the Kikuyu tribe of that region.

The students had a good basic knowledge of English and some experience in teaching in schools, but the historical, cultural and conceptual background of modern systems of education was new to them. It had no relationship with their tribal ways of upbringing and preparation for adult life. The curriculum in those days provided no opportunity to bridge this gap. I had read Jomo Kenyatta's (he was to later become the first President of independent Kenya) fascinating account of the Kikuyu way of life in his book *Facing Mount Kenya* (1938), based on his doctoral thesis under the anthropologist Bronislaw Malinowski at the University of London. I had also read Elspeth Huxley's *Red Strangers* (1939), a novel about the coming of white settlers in Kenya's highlands and how they were perceived by Kikuyu tribals. Despite being an outsider, I took an interest in the students' home conditions. During teaching practice, we had to visit village schools for the purpose of observation. There we saw women at work, carrying fuelwood, digging, clearing land, drawing water, cooking and selling produce in roadside markets.

In our teaching, however, there was no scope for local studies. The curriculum, textbooks, etc., had all been designed and prepared in the UK and had to be followed. The medium of instruction was English. Swahili, the lingua franca of East Africa, was taught as one of the subjects. The main course was of two years' duration for primary school teaching. There were also short-term refresher courses for secondary school teachers.

Among extracurricular activities, I led two climbing trips on Mount Kenya with the help of an experienced African guide. We took the route on the western side along Mackinder Valley, named after the explorer, Harold Mackinder, who reached the summit towards the end of the nineteenth century, starting from the base camp at Naru Moro. We traversed through a thick equatorial forest, an open deciduous belt, bamboo forest, coniferous trees, an alpine grassland, and ended at the snout of a glacier lined with weathered rocks. The highest peaks could be seen in the distance. The night was spent in a small wooden hut, tucked into our sleeping bags, with temperatures well below freezing point. The next day, after getting up early, we walked some distance on the side of the glacier toward the peaks, reaching a height of 15,000 or so feet. Climbing the peaks required special equipment, which we did not have. We returned the same day to the base camp and took the bus to Nyeri. As part of my geography teaching, I organised field visits to tea and coffee plantations and factories.

Among other memorable events from this time was a visit by Kenya's President, Jomo Kenyatta, to Nyeri. There was a huge gathering of mainly Kikuyu tribals, dressed in their ochre wraparounds. They occupied the main streets up to the shop fronts, where we stood with our cameras to catch a glimpse of and photograph the great Mzee, who had led Kenya's freedom struggle and had spent many years in jail. He arrived standing in an open sedan car, smiling and waving at delirious crowds with his monkey tail hair fly-whisk. Kikuyu women greeted him with their traditional ululating sounds. He made a short speech in Swahili, encouraging people to unite and work hard for the progress of the country. Despite the large numbers, there was no chaos. However, the wife of one of our Canadian colleagues found the heat and crowds exhausting and nearly passed out. Later, while talking about the experience, she described it as being in the midst of 'a mass of creepy, crawling creatures'. Clearly, she had yet to understand the humanity of the people her husband had come to work for.

Another event was the friendly hockey match between a team from Pakistan and a Nyeri team, composed mostly of other Asians. We were no match for them. They ran circles around us and scored at will. We went down 12–1 or so.

In June that year, India's Prime Minister, Pandit Jawaharlal Nehru, passed away. I heard the news on the radio and broke down sobbing. That day, I did not eat and just sat listening to mournful music and tributes on All India Radio. That experience made me realise my deep attachment to India and her destiny that Panditji had done so much to define and shape after her independence from British rule.

Nyeri was a market town and therefore had a sizeable trading community of Gujaratis, who celebrated the national nine-day Mother Goddess festival, Navratri, with Garba dancing. Sudesh and I joined these festivities in traditional Indian dress and learnt Garba. The few Punjabis in Nyeri were saw millers, contractors and transporters. There was also a well-stocked bookshop owned by the Mahajan family, catering to British settlers and educational institutions.

A few months after our marriage, Sudesh's parents, her brother Naresh and his daughter Rena visited us in Nyeri. We showed them around. They were happy to see our home, Kagumo College and the work I was involved in. After they left, Sudesh discovered that she was pregnant and started on a prenatal care regime. Unfortunately, she had a miscarriage and had to be hospitalised for a couple of days. She remained depressed for a while, but soon recovered her spirits, with support and care from the wives of colleagues and from Urmilla and Neves when they visited from Nairobi.

Another rather nasty experience was that our car was caught in stone-pelting by crowds while returning from a film show. It was late in the evening and pitch dark. Foolishly, I stopped the car, opened the door and, standing on the chassis on the driver's side, started shouting at the crowd. Suddenly, a van came at high speed from the opposite direction and hit the open door behind me. Instinctively, I pushed my stomach against the edge of the car roof, bearing the brunt of the door's impact on my back. Apparently, I had left the headlights on, which had blinded the van's driver who was trying to escape from the stone-pelting crowd. The next day, seeing the wrecked condition of my car, the repair shop staff marvelled at my luck at getting away unhurt by the accident. We escaped this mishap unscathed, but a greater tragedy lay ahead.

Mrs Bohannon, who had been Prem's landlady in London and was like a mother to him, came to visit us in November 1964. Among other things, we took her for a night's stay at Treetops, a wooden lodge built atop a huge tree, overlooking a waterhole in the thick equatorial rainforest at the foot of Mount Kenya. To approach the lodge, guests had to walk along a path for the last several hundred yards of the journey, escorted by an experienced white hunter whose job it was to ward off wild animals. Then, they had to climb a staircase to reach the lodge, 80 feet above the ground. There we were allotted rooms and served dinner in a common dining hall. Below, at the waterhole, there were processions of wild animals—boars, elephants, blackbuck, leopard, buffaloes—that could be viewed in safety.

Most of the time, Mrs Bohannon was happy to stay at home and talk with us about spiritual matters, especially in the Hindu tradition. One day, she cooked pork chops for dinner. We ate together and after listening to some music, retired for the night. Around midnight, Mrs Bohannon felt uneasy and began to vomit. Seeing that her condition was worsening, we took her to hospital. She was there for a couple of days and seemed to be recovering, so we brought her home. But she had a relapse and was unable to retain food. Mrs Bohannon had to be hospitalised again. However, since her condition did not improve, she had to be shifted to Nairobi Hospital. Both these hospitals were the best available in Kenya. Prem came to be with her a few times but could not do much as Raksha, his wife, had just given birth to their son, Sanjay. Around the same time, in December, we had been booked to go on long leave to India.

We saw Mrs Bohannon for the last time in hospital under intensive care. She gave us a kind look and raised her hand to bless us. We stood there, utterly helpless. After we left, her husband arrived from England. In spite of all efforts by the hospital staff, she did not respond to treatment and passed away. John Bohannon flew back to England with the body. We got the news in India. It was a terrible shock for all of us. It took us a long time to recover from guilt and remorse at the fact that a dear friend should have come to such an end while staying with us. Our friends Neves and Urmilla Pereira, then in Nairobi, were angry with us for going on holiday and leaving our guest in such a dire condition. Neves called us 'lousy friends'. For many years after that, they cut us off.

I have often thought about these incidents, trying to figure out right and wrong on our part. Now, I feel that we should have postponed our holidays and stayed in Nairobi to give moral and emotional support to Mrs Bohannon and John in their hour of distress. That would have been the right thing to do. However, the combination of circumstances, systems, our own inclinations and the working of some design beyond our ken led to what actually happened, had to happen, was destined to happen (होनी).

5

India

December 1964–February 1965

We arrived in Bombay in late December. Nilambari Chopatkat, Sudesh's friend from her days in Uganda, had arranged for us to stay with her family in the Malabar Hill area. They were the erstwhile rulers of the princely state (Rajwada) of Mansa in north Gujarat during the British colonial regime. After independence, the state was merged with the Republic of India. Nilambari's uncle, Shri Himmatsinh of Mansa, was the Chairman of Associated Cement Company, a private concern, and an important political figure close to the Indian National Congress (INC), the ruling party. I had long conversations with him over morning cups of tea and also read the major daily newspapers. This gave me some idea of the evolving post-Nehru politics in India. I shared with him my desire to return to India and live and work here. He was on the governing board of Mayo College in Ajmer. He introduced me to Mr Jack Gibson, who was the principal at the time, to explore a possible opportunity for me to work with him. During our stay in Bombay we did some sightseeing and attended cultural events like *qawwali* performances. Sudesh was treated as a daughter of the family. I think by associating with other daughters, aunts and mothers, she acquired some of the grace, poise and sense of self-importance characteristic of Rajput princesses.

While in the area I made a visit to Mahatma Gandhi's ashram at Sevagram. There I met Aryanayakam and Ashadevi, who were conducting teacher training for *Nai Taalim* or Basic

Education,[1] the alternative method of education visualised by Gandhiji to replace the system put in place by Macaulay. They were kind and gracious in sharing their views and encouraging me to consider returning to India to join them. I also experienced firsthand the ashram routine of multi-faith prayers in the early morning and evening, physical labour, spinning, teaching children and helping with cooking, cleaning and other maintenance tasks. After three days in the austere community of Gandhiji's disciples, who were devoted to realising his dream of Sarvodaya (Upliftment of All) based on self-reliant, self-governing village republics, I returned to Bombay, the bustling, hustling commercial metropolis of modernising India. After 10 days in the house in Malabar Hill, our hosts decided to give us some privacy and arranged for us to stay in a flat on our own. After spending another week in Bombay we took the train to Ajmer on our way to Delhi, Uttar Pradesh and Punjab to visit our relatives.

As I mentioned earlier, Shri Himmatsinh had introduced us to Mr Gibson, Principal of Mayo College, Ajmer. We spent a couple of days there, staying in the College guest house. Mr Gibson took us around and showed us the teaching, residential and sports facilities of this prestigious institution, built by the British for the scions of the royal families of Rajputana, now Rajasthan. The buildings combined Victorian and Rajput motifs in their architecture. There were spacious sports grounds. The principal lived in a large mansion befitting his status. Mr Gibson had begun his career as a teacher and rose to become the head. He was very English, not only in his accent but also in his ideas of education. He considered it his task to prepare future rulers for India by replicating the patterns of English public schools. The College was now open to non-Rajput students. It also took merit into consideration and provided scholarships for the needy. Mr Gibson could not offer any prospect of work in the near future, but asked me to stay in touch with him. Later, I met him in London in

1967. As it happened, our son was admitted to Mayo College in 1977 and studied there for seven years, till the end of senior secondary school in 1984.

From Ajmer, we took the train to Delhi to stay with Sudesh's Mama (maternal uncle), Mr Kundan Lal Rampal. He was a master tailor who had worked for a reputed British clothier in Lahore. After Partition, he had moved to Delhi and become a partner in the business with a shop in Connaught Place. He had a flat nearby, above the then-famous York Restaurant. He stayed there with his wife and two children—his son Anil and daughter Pawan. They welcomed us in their midst, treating us to the sights, cinemas, *chaat* and savouries of Delhi.

During our stay in Delhi we visited my grandfather, Bhaayaji, and family living in Paharganj in a two-room house in a narrow *gali* (by-lane), which had earlier been occupied by Muslim families who had moved to Pakistan. Bhaayaji had moved there from Rawalpindi as a refugee. He was given this temporary accommodation while he awaited an allotment of land in Rajendra Nagar. We negotiated the narrow streets with its open sewage drains, dodging showers of water and garbage from the upper floors, to reach a doorway that led into a small courtyard, with a staircase leading to a terrace. Bhaayaji sat there on a charpai, basking in the hazy winter sun, and Maasi, his second wife, was seated on the floor preparing the morning meal. We bowed and touched their feet as a mark of our respect. I sat with Bhaayaji while Sudesh sat on a stool near Maasi. Maasi opened the conversation in her high-pitched nasal drone: '*Kadi aaye o, ki laaye o?*' ('When did you arrive, what have you brought?') We had not brought anything and said something unconvincing in response. Bhaayaji launched into a sermon on filial duties towards elders, including the imperative of carrying gifts while visiting them. We felt guilty and listened in polite silence. Maasi insisted we eat with them. I had grown up listening to stories, mostly negative, about stepmothers, including the mythic tale of Kekayi, King Dashrath's fourth wife, who had insisted on exile for Lord Rama so that her son, Bharata, could be crowned as Ayodhya's ruler. In our extended family, stepmothers had been part of the family across generations. I had experienced my own share of suffering at the hands of my stepmother. On this occasion, Maasi served us her special *kheer* (rice pudding), moong dal and *bhartha*. It was touching to see this tender side of Maasi, whom I had always feared and disliked. After the meal, we took their leave. I gave Bhaayaji Rs 500 as a parting gift.

Our other obligatory visit in Delhi was to my maternal uncle, 'Little' Mama (the term we all used), and his family in Rajendra Nagar. During my childhood, many of my school vacations had been spent in my maternal home in Peshawar, where I was born. After my mother's early death, my aunts on this side of the family looked after us. Amongst them, Little Mama's wife, Parameshwari, was especially fond of us. Even though she already had three or four children of her own, she treated us like her own. We all called her Bibiji. Little Mama was the tallest in the family. We never understood why he was called 'Little'. He was also the most affectionate and self-effacing, ready to care for and serve others. In Peshawar, he worked with my maternal grandfather or Nanaji, Dr Badrinath Jaitly, as a compounder, preparing and dispensing prescriptions. After arriving in Delhi post the Partition, my Mamaji had been helped by the Malhotra family to set up a charitable dispensary adjacent to their transport business on Roshanara Road. Before 1947, the Malhotras used to run a bus service from Peshawar into the tribal areas of the North Western Frontier Province. They were regular visitors to our home in Peshawar, always with bags full of dry fruits as gifts. They also carried cartons of Lifebuoy soap and other goods for sale to frontier villages. Now they were emerging as major transporters in north India, under the name of Jaipur Golden Transport Company.

Years later, after our return to India in 1972, the owner of Jaipur Golden Transport, Kishenlal Malhotra, came to see us in Udaipur. One of the women in the family, now in her 80s, still comes for walks along Fatehsagar. I always make it a point to stop and talk to her. She remembers my Nana, Lal Mama and Little Mama. She also talks about how lucrative their transportation business was in Peshawar, with bagfuls of earnings in cash brought from interior areas. Her husband, Tilak Raj Malhotra, had done his internship under Lal Mama, a qualified doctor.

We were going to meet Little Mama and his family after nearly twenty years. I had last seen him in May 1949, when he came to see us off at Delhi railway station as Beji, Prem and I set out for Kenya. Bibiji was overwhelmed to see me. With tears in her eyes, she drew me close, pouring love, sadness, pity and joy into her warm embrace and singsong voice. Then she hugged Sudesh and greeted her with blessings for a happy married life. She served us food prepared in her own Peshawari style and told us about her children. The oldest and only daughter, Santosh, whom we called Toshibehnji, was married to an army officer, Colonel Sudan. Narendra was in Bombay, working with legendary theatre and film actor Prithvi Raj Kapoor. Peshi and Ravi had joined the Indian Navy. Kishore was training for the Indian Air Force. The youngest, Arun, was still at school. She also told us about other members of my maternal family, now scattered across north India. Bibiji was regarded as the central hub to whom all felt connected and welcome. We were able to get the addresses of Kako Maasi and Narendra for a future visit.

After several fun-filled days of reconnecting in Delhi's as-yet unpolluted, hazy sunshine, we headed north to Dehradun with Rampal Mamaji and his family, packed in his vintage

Buick, driven by a daredevil of a driver. For the most part, the road was a single tarmac track. It was nighttime and there was a constant stream of trucks, sugarcane-laden bullock carts and the odd bus. Everyone hogged the tarmac, giving minimum way at the last moment to oncoming vehicles. Being used to a more disciplined and considerate driving, the journey was a nightmare for us, as we feared a head-on collision with the passing of each vehicle. For our hosts, all this was normal, and they dozed, unperturbed. After nearly nine hours, we reached our destination early in the morning.

In Dehradun, the days were spent in a leisurely fashion. We would get up late to hot tea served in bed, *aloo*, *mooli* or *gobi* parathas for breakfast, munching on raw carrots and radish at midday, a late lunch, evening walks in the bazaars, and evenings spent sitting around the wood fire and chatting. On one of those days, it snowed in Mussoorie. So we drove up to see the snow-clad shops and the mall. On another day I took Anil and Pawan for a hike along a mule track to Rajpur, 7 miles up from Dehradun.

Sudesh and I made a day trip to Haridwar, situated on the banks of the Ganga, the venue of our annual pilgrimage as children with Beji and her sister-in-law, Mayadevi from Gheloki. As I stood on Har Ki Paudhi watching the powerful flow of the sacred river, an urge arose from the depths of my being for a holy dip, even though the water was freezing cold. On an impulse, I undressed and took three dips in the river. Emerging from the water, I felt a kind of warmth within and a sense of having been reborn after immersing myself in this ancient mother stream of Indian civilisation.

Back in Dehradun, there were also some homely lessons for me as a son-in-law. A family astrologer read my palm and predicted that I was destined to perform great tasks in life. I found this both intriguing and disconcerting. I talked to Mamaji about my intention to return and work for India.

He advised against it, saying that the conditions here were not conducive to good work. To ensure a comfortable and decent life, we should stay abroad. Apparently, after moving to Delhi, he himself had suffered losses in business at the hands of people he had helped and trusted.

From Dehradun, we took the train to Jalandhar. There we spent a couple of days with Lal Mamaji and his family. He was a trained doctor, but had become an alcoholic after his dislocation from Peshawar. His wife, my Mamiji, who was admired and envied as the most beautiful of our aunts, carried on heroically to take care of him and bring up their three daughters and son. The girls were quite bright, helping their mother and each other. We also met Shivji Chacha with his family, as well as Chacha Shanti Prakash, who was unmarried. They too were going through hard times after Partition.

Our next and last stop in Punjab was Amritsar, where we visited Rameshwar Chacha and his family. He was working there as an excise and taxation officer. He believed in honesty in his occupation and enjoyed the respect of the traders he dealt with. They lived in a large two-storeyed house with rooms and verandas built around an inner courtyard, which was shared by several families. They had moved there from West Punjab after the Partition. We stayed there for three days, fitting in visits to the Golden Temple, Durgiana Mandir and Jallianwala Bagh.

From Amritsar, we took the train to Jhansi to visit Kako Maasi, her husband Sagar and their two young boys. Sagar was an officer in the Indian Army. They lived in a well-furnished bungalow with modern facilities and orderlies. They were extremely affectionate and showed us around the forts and palaces of Maratha rulers in Jhansi and Orchha. We also heard the local legends of Jhansi Ki Rani, the queen who had fought against the East India Company's army during the 1857 rebellion, which is sometimes referred to as India's first war of independence. I also learnt that the famous temples of Khajuraho, with their erotic sculptures, were only an overnight train journey away. Since Sudesh was sick, I decided to go there alone, leaving Sudesh in their care. In Khajuraho, I spent the whole day looking around the remarkably well-preserved Hindu and Jain temples, with their exquisite and explicit statues and bas-reliefs of gods, goddesses, *yaksha*s and animals in amorous, erotic postures. I took many slides and photographs on my small Canon camera. I took the train back to Jhansi the same night. On my return, I found Sudesh in a miserable condition. Being sick, she had no appetite, but Kako Maasi insisted on feeding her with her own hands. Those who knew Maasi had learnt to escape her ministrations, but Sudesh did not know how to cope with it. She was relieved to see me and settled down for the rest of our stay. The children kept us amused with their games, questions and performances. Sagar had a wide range of interests and engaged me in long spiritual and philosophical conversations. He also wanted to know what people abroad thought about India and what life was like there. Perhaps he had in mind the possibility of sending the boys abroad to study, which was not an uncommon aspiration among educated, middle-class Indians.

Back in Bombay, we stayed at the Sea Green Hotel on Marine Drive. Himmatsinhji had arranged this for us as his guests. We had a splendid view of the ocean and ample opportunity for walks along the Marine Drive seashore. We also visited the museums and art galleries. I was also able to make a visit to Poona to meet my friend, Chandrashekhar Sastry, from our Birmingham days. Finally, after a week or so, we bade farewell to our hosts and took the flight back to Nairobi.

ENDNOTES

1. The four principles of Nai Talim were: an emphasis on education in the mother tongue as well as handicraft-based skills and work; work based in the locality; a vocational approach to learning; and socially useful and constructive work. See https://journalsofindia.com/nai-talim/ (accessed 2 June 2023).

6

Kenya

1965–68

Back in Nyeri, we began our life anew in a spacious bungalow for senior staff, with a large garden in front and a plot for growing vegetables at the back. In June I suffered a serious bout of viral 'flu that kept me in bed for over a week. This seemed to have annoyed the Principal, Mr Popkin, who thought I was avoiding work. After I recovered, I put in extra effort to clear the backlog of teaching. The end of the year saw the departure of Mr Popkin and the appointment of an African Principal, Alexander Mina Getao, a tall, well-built figure with the kindly but authoritative demeanour of a tribal chief. We got along well. He entrusted me with more responsibilities, like coordinating staff meetings, syllabus preparation and holding examinations. During this time a group of American educators visited the college and we had opportunity to discuss approaches to education with them, with a special focus on the problem of community vis-à-vis the individual. I argued for education that inculcated responsibility to the community. According to one of the visitors, an expert in the sociology of education, the community could be oppressive even in a modern industrial society like America. Therefore, according to him, the emphasis in education had to be on safeguarding individuality.

In August, Sudesh became pregnant again. This time she was more careful and avoided unnecessary intervention. We decided to forgo long travel, settling into a congenial routine of listening to music, knitting, reading, morning and evening walks, and wholesome meals. The company of my colleagues' wives who had already experienced motherhood—June Gillespie, Lou Sharp, Evelyn Downey, Mrs Getao—was a great source of support for Sudesh. Our Kikuyu cook, Wachira, was also of great help, making sure Sudesh ate properly and on time. He had his own advice about prenatal dos and don'ts.

On 5 March 1966, Sudesh felt the early signs of labour. I took her to Mount Kenya Hospital, where she was examined by Dr Patel who decided to admit Sudesh immediately. There was no provision for husbands to stay overnight, so I returned home in the evening. The next morning, I was woken by a call from the hospital telling me the baby had come and that it was a boy. I rushed to the hospital. Entering the delivery room, I saw Sudesh lying on the bed with the baby next to her. She looked divinely content and asked me if I was happy it was a boy. Of course I was, and I would have been equally so had it been a girl. We had already thought of the name Tarun. We had chosen 'Tarun' for its poetic and literary resonance in Bengali and Sanskrit. It was only later that we discovered that it stood for youth and uprightness. Its root is 'Taru', which means 'tree'.

A week later, I brought Sudesh and Tarun home. It was an uncanny experience, having another presence in the house, so small but so full of vitality and promise, such a source of joy with just a wisp of a smile, fully trusting, commanding total attention, care and love. Our whole life was changed to revolve around the needs of the newborn. Sudesh began breastfeeding for a few days but could not sustain it for long, and bottle feeding was started. We realised the importance of breastfeeding to bolster immunity much later. I played my part in feeding the baby and keeping him clean. An important change occurred in our relationship. There was less tension and more understanding and mutuality. After a few days, the families of colleagues came visiting, laden with gifts. As Tarun grew older, children came home to play with him as well. And so the time went by, filled with the wondrous appearance of new movements, moods and sounds in the house.

In December, we received a phone call from Jinja about the sudden demise of Sudesh's father, Hans Raj Sharma. She was distraught. We left immediately for Jinja via Nairobi, where Prem joined us. We drove all night to reach in time for the cremation. Amidst all the stress and confusion Tarun, who was only nine months old at the time, fell ill with severe diarrhoea and had to be taken to the hospital. We stayed with him all night, giving him spoonfuls of water laced with electrolytes. He kept fading away, but continued to sip water. Our hearts swung between prayer and despair. Around four in the morning he opened his eyes and began to show increasing vitality. We too regained hope and kept up the treatment. The diarrhoea finally stopped and he made a quick recovery. After a few days in the hospital and at home in Jinja, we returned to Nyeri.

In January 1967, I requested a posting in Mombasa to enable Father, who had been living alone, to stay with us. A new educational institute called the Coast Teacher Training College had come up at Shanzu, north of Mombasa. I was asked to join there after the holidays.

This new institution had been recently constructed atop an old raised coral reef along the coast. The buildings and houses on this new site had a modern design and were made entirely of concrete. We were first allotted a single storey, two-bedroom quarter with ground-level vents in the walls. All amenities at home had to be set up from scratch. Father came to stay with us. An ayah was engaged to help with looking after Tarun. He got along well with his grandfather, whom he called Pitaji. They went out for walks around the campus and played games. Father read to him and told him stories. One day, as Tarun was playing on the floor, he noticed four mamba snakelets wriggling along in a corner. He followed them, but before he could reach them, I spotted the creatures and pulled him back. They had just hatched and had come in through the open vents. The episode gave us a scare and soon after that, we moved to a new two-storey house with a spacious area in front that we converted into a lawn.

As at Kagumo, the college had a multiracial staff with people from British, American, Asian and African backgrounds. The Principal, Frank Bentley, recognised this and gave space and support to everyone. Since it was a new initiative that aimed to complete in two years the training for full-time teachers in primary education, every aspect—curriculum, schedules, teaching aids, textbooks, library, extra-curricular activities—had to be planned and organised from scratch. An academic staff committee was set up, chaired by the Principal. Mr Bentley asked me to be its convenor. This was exciting work that gave me an opportunity to introduce new ideas and content. It was also a challenge to take into account and integrate the views and suggestions of staff with diverse backgrounds.

Amongst the topics I introduced in educational psychology was child development. I did this by encouraging students to observe their own and their neighbours' children at different ages and record the changes. However, my most ambitious undertaking was a local study project involving all the staff and students for three weeks on a full-time basis. This is how it came about.

In 1967, a decision was made to introduce a three-term pattern for the academic year. This was to be done in the middle of the year. The change left us with a three-week gap in which something had to be done to keep staff and students engaged. I suggested devoting this time to studying the region in which the College was located in a systematic way. A sub-regional framework was visualised, starting from the sea in the east and extending through the coral reef, beach, fossil reef and floodplain, to the low hills in the west.

These north–south strips had to be studied by the students on an inter-disciplinary basis, both in the field and through library work. This was to be done in the format of a project, guided by the staff. The main subject areas for study were geography, history, science, mathematics, social studies, economy and culture.

Students across classes were divided into groups and sub-groups, keeping this matrix of sub-regions and subjects in mind. The first week was given to library work and planning. This was followed by nine days of fieldwork. During this time, students spoke to local farmers, fisher-folk and factory workers to learn about their occupations and culture. They collected samples of crops, fruit, crafts, shells, coral and rocks. Those with a camera took photographs. Others drew sketches and paintings of what they saw. The concluding five days were given to writing reports, sketching, making charts and hanging displays for an exhibition of the work done. The editor of a local English newspaper, the *Mombasa Times*, was invited to inaugurate the display. He was so impressed, he wrote an editorial in the next day's edition, applauding the effort and recommending it as a creative approach in education. I suggested to the Principal that the college could invite practising teachers from schools to come and see the work and have a discussion on it, but he disagreed and the display was taken down the very next day. However, the staff and students appreciated having this opportunity to work together and get to know each other and the locality better.

While I carried on with my duties in the college, Sudesh was fully occupied with Tarun, assisted by the ayah, a young Kamba girl. In February 1967, Sudesh was pregnant again. This was unplanned but we decided to maintain it. Since we were close to the beach, we spent weekends there, taking children, towels, beach umbrellas and packed lunch with us. Prem and Raksha, along with baby Sanjay and Shaila, visited us during the holidays, as did Anwar Sheikh, his wife

Musharraf and their daughters Mahira and Shama. Since we lived 15 miles north of Mombasa, we could not be a part of the social life there, but we did make friends with some of the residents in the Nyali Beach area, among them Dr Zarina Patel and her husband. Zarina hosted regular discussion sessions on topical issues, to which she invited visiting scholars. It was there that we met a group of American students from the Friends World College (FWC), led by Lee Haring, their faculty adviser. As we shall see, this encounter was to prove fateful in giving a new direction to our lives and ways of thought.

In July, my long leave became due. This time we chose to go to England to stay with Sudesh's older sister Pushpa, her husband Lakhpat Rai and their son Deepak. They lived near Wimbledon in London. Sudesh felt very close to her sister, who had taken care of her during their mother's frequent illnesses. Pushpa and Lakhpat had left Uganda and settled in England. They both had teaching jobs. They accepted us as part of their family, but we soon saw the strains in their relationship. Lakhpat spent his evenings drinking in pubs. He would come home late and demand hot meals. Pushpa refused to oblige. There was shouting and quarrels, and Deepak would hide under the bed. Lakhpat usually ended up making butter-laced parathas for himself. He ate while talking amiably to me. In the beginning, I tried to intervene and counsel them. But it was futile. They had got into a pattern of quarrelling at night and making up in the morning. On holidays, we took the children for walks in Wimbledon Park. I even managed to watch some matches at the famous Wimbledon tennis courts during the English Open Tennis Championships that year.

Taking advantage of being in London, I began exploring the possibility of continuing my postgraduate studies in education. I had been introduced to the work of Arnold Gesell, Jean Piaget and B. F. Skinner in the field of child development through the educational psychology course in the M. Ed. programme at Birmingham. I had become especially interested in the cognitive aspect of child development, so I prepared a research proposal to study cognitive development in children from non-Western cultures. I discussed my ideas with Dr Ruth Beard, one of my lecturers in Birmingham, who had shifted to the Institute of Education, University of London. She helped me to finalise my proposal and recommended my application for a PhD in Education at the Institute, with Professor P. E. Vernon as my guide. It was accepted. I completed the paperwork for registration, paid the fees, met Professor Vernon and began my preliminary reading in the library. This involved daily visits from Wimbledon to Russell Square where the institute was located, within the School of Oriental and African Studies. It was agreed that my field research would be in Kenya with African children. My broad hypothesis was that the nature of cognition and patterns of cognitive growth were likely to be different in non-Western cultures. I proposed to test this using methodology developed by Jean Piaget.

During this time I saw an advertisement for the position of a lecturer in education at the University of Dar-e-Salaam. I decided to apply and gave the names of W. D. Craig, Dr Ruth Beard and Harold Loukes as referees. To my surprise, I was called for an interview, to be held at University of Bristol. I had some familiarity with Tanganyika and the ideas of African Socialism advanced by its charismatic President, Julius Nyerere, through his book *Uhuru na Ujamaa*, or *Freedom and Solidarity* (1968). I refreshed my knowledge on this and its implications for education. At the interview, there was a panel of fifteen academics, mostly from Britain, together with a representative of the Government of Tanganyika. Apparently, I was the only candidate. I dealt as best as I could with this formidable presence, but my performance was not good enough, especially as regards my command of Swahili, the official language of the country. I was not selected, but it was an interesting experience which made me realise that perhaps I did not have the aptitude for a purely academic career.

In August, we decided to take a holiday in Europe. We booked a tour to the ski resort of Kitzbuehl in the Austrian Alps. We stayed in a mid-range hotel, spending our time taking walks in the countryside, carrying Tarun on my back in a *papoose*, watching Tyrollean dancing and making ski lift excursions to the higher ranges. At meal times, 1-year-old Tarun sat with us for a while, but would then wander off to other tables. Most guests were tolerant, but some felt annoyed and frowned at us. We would remember this difference in attitude towards children in public places in Europe in comparison with those in Africa, the Americas and India.

7

Kenya

1967–68

After this excursion, it was time to return to my duties in Kenya. Sudesh was close to term by then. On reaching Nairobi from London, we decided that she should stay there with Prem and Raksha since I had to set up our new house at Shanzu. Sudesh gave birth to our daughter, Amita, on 11 September 1967 in a missionary hospital. Tarun was left with Prem and his family, which was rather hard for him at that age, despite the love and care given by Raksha and Prem. Three days after Amita was born, they took him to see Sudesh. Children were not allowed inside the hospital, so he could only see Sudesh through a window. This upset him badly. He would not stop crying. Only with great effort were Prem and Raksha able to calm him. I reached Nairobi a couple of weeks later and we all drove back to our new home at Shanzu.

In December 1967, Sudesh and I, along with the children, drove to Nairobi in my Fiat 1100 to spend the holidays with Prem and Raksha. Along the way, the car's windscreen was shattered by a pebble thrown up by a passing vehicle. No one was hurt. We stopped, cleared the broken glass and continued our journey. We had to drive slower and so were delayed. At dusk, near the junction to Machakos, a policeman standing away from the road waved at the car. Assuming that he was asking for a ride, I carried on driving. A few miles ahead, a police vehicle overtook us and asked us to stop. Two policemen with guns came over, dragged me out and began hitting me. I put my arms around my head to shield myself from serious hurt. They were talking in their own language, so I couldn't make out what was happening. After a while, they asked me about the windscreen and whether it was shattered because I had hit someone while driving. I explained what had happened. I also told them I was a government servant. But they did not believe me. They asked me to drive to the police station in Nairobi with one of them sitting in the front seat. Sudesh, the children and the ayah sat at the back.

When we reached Nairobi police station, I was asked to walk along a straight line and do other exercises to see if I was under the influence of alcohol. After some paperwork, they allowed me to call Prem, who came over and took us home. Our car was kept at the police station. It was well beyond midnight when we reached Prem and Raksha's home. The children were fed and put to bed. Then we talked about the ordeal and what was to be done. I retrieved the car the next day and got it repaired. With Prem's help, I also engaged a lawyer for the case. Back in Shanzu, I resumed my duties. We tried to carry on with life as before, but something inside me had changed.

Around the same time, there were major upheavals afoot in government policies. Rapid Africanisation had begun for the lower ranks of the railway and civil services, hitherto manned by Asians.[1] They were given the choice of taking up Kenyan citizenship or early retirement. Almost all of them had British citizenship. The majority among them opted to retain this and take early retirement from government service. This set in motion what came to be known as the Asian Exodus of 1968.[2] Most of them moved to Britain. Some went to Canada. Very few went back to India or Pakistan. Being in the top grade of the education service, there was no pressure on me in this matter, but we could not remain unaffected by these events.

A few months later, the case came up for hearing at a court in Machakos. The police had by then identified the vehicle which had hit a pedestrian, leading to his death, but I did not know this. I went for the hearing accompanied by my lawyer, with the children's ayah as witness. The charge was that I had not stopped when asked to do so by a traffic official on duty. My plea was that the policeman who tried to wave us down was standing well away from the road and was not clearly visible in the dusk. The ayah confirmed that she had seen policemen pulling me out and beating me. However, the British magistrate ignored all this, found me guilty and imposed a fine of 500 Kenyan shillings. I paid the amount and the case was closed. But the whole experience was disheartening. It led to doubts about whether we'd ever be accepted as ourselves in the new Kenya.

Through the year I had kept in touch with Lee Haring of the Friends World College, New York. He invited me to lead discussions with the students. I spoke to them about the historical background and geographical features of Kenya and East Africa, as also about the education system that I was part of. From them, I learnt about the social and political upheavals of the 1960s in the USA, especially the students' protests and campus unrest, to which their college was trying to provide an answer. This resonated with my own unease with the colonial system of education I was trained in and was perpetuating. At one point, Lee suggested I think about joining Friends World College. I shared this with Sudesh and Father. There were many aspects to be considered. Father would have to live alone again, at least for a while, as Prem was also planning to go to the United States for further studies. I'd be leaving a permanent and pensionable job to move to a temporary position in a new venture in education with an uncertain future. It would be a whole new way of life to adjust to in a new country. On the other hand, our unsavoury encounter with the prevailing system of law and order in Kenya tipped the scales towards my taking early retirement and our leaving Kenya. Of course, there was the exciting prospect of a new experience and the opening up of new vistas of knowledge. My inner voice reminded me of my tryst with India and questioned this move westwards. I justified this choice by telling myself that it was only a temporary venture to see for myself the twentieth century at the peak of its progress.

I told Lee Haring about my decision and gave him the basics of my biodata, which he forwarded to New York with a strong recommendation. In no time the appointment letter and immigration papers arrived. I went to the US embassy in Nairobi for our visas. It was striking to see the relaxed, friendly atmosphere there, without the stuffiness of colonial British bureaucracy. The consul himself took me to his office, completed the formalities and issued visas. Back in Mombasa, I submitted my three months' notice of resignation and requested the paid leave due to me with sea passage to the UK. Once this was approved, we began preparing for departure. With the help of a Sindhi friend, a place was found in Mombasa for Father to stay. The car and all our belongings, except for essential clothing and books, were disposed of.

Along with my college duties, I had tried to carry on research for my doctoral work. I had designed questionnaires and, with the help of local teachers, began testing them on children from nearby African schools. I also continued reading research-related books that I had brought from England. Now I wrote to my guide, Professor Vernon, about the change in our circumstances. He understood our desire to seek safe haven in the USA and advised me to postpone my research while maintaining my registration with the London University Institute of Education. This would, however, lapse after a few years. Thus, having the tag of 'Doctor' before my name would never come about, despite reminders and urging from Prem. Perhaps it was my disenchantment with formal scholarship that led to it.

The Principal arranged a farewell gathering at his home. In his speech, he mentioned that I was ranked second in the shortlist of candidates for the position he was holding. Other colleagues also spoke warmly of my stint in the college. I thanked everyone for their friendship and cooperation. Later, Mr Bentley wrote a testimonial highlighting my contribution to integrating and grounding the diverse streams that had been brought together in this new college. These are his words:

> Mr Saint had served this College with sufficient enthusiasm to leave behind an impression which one hopes will permeate the academic work for a long time to come. His own academic training, which is considerable, has left a decisive mark on his approach to work in the College; his inquisitive approach to methodology has at times contrasted with the more traditional concepts of other tutors, thus producing a healthy dialogue in matters of approach to subject and students. He has always been willing to partake in advisory staff committees on a variety of topics, and he has invariably made a worthwhile contribution. In our early days he joined a staff committee which gave careful thought to scheduling and as a result we have been able to evolve programmes directed in terms of the climatic and physical conditions of this new environment.
>
> As a colleague, Mr Saint has earned considerable respect for his reasonable, sincere and thoughtful attitudes to people; clearly this was a situation in which these qualities were at a premium. The staff is composed of elements from three previous Colleges, and of teachers from the main racial groupings in the country. There were, in addition, the religious traditions of these separate Colleges to add to the heterogeneity. In all these potential difficulties, I have been aware of Mr Saint's influence in encouraging a friendly interchange of ideas and a gradual welding of purpose within the staff group.

Although now well-qualified and experienced in diverse educational situations, Mr Saint has commenced further studies for his doctorate. I fully expect that educational thought will eventually benefit from the published product of many years of his diligent work.

F. J. Bentley, Principal

Students also organised a send-off. One of them wrote a letter conveying his appreciation, feelings and good wishes:

I feel it fitting at this time of personal gratitude and sorrow, especially when one has to leave others to take up new appointment in another country, and with regard to your services which this poor country admires, and especially myself. I am, therefore, obliged, Sir, to say that your departure is a great potential threat to the educational future of this poor country. And if I am allowed to say, I should be delighted to mention how secure I felt under you, as we need to work with trust, respect and honour, it was indeed amicable. And to lose one with such top qualities is a great blow.

I wish to express my gratitude for your enthusiasm and initiative you have shown in our educational progress. I must also say that every one of us has valued and admired your principles, that these days in schools we speak of 'SAINT'S METHOD'.

ZAKARIA ODUA OMONDY
STUDENT

Just before our departure, a few family friends in Mombasa invited us to their homes to give us their blessings for the new career we were embarking upon.

This marked the end of 20 years of my life in Kenya and England. This is where I grew from an unruly, wilful adolescent to a self-confident, mature adult; from a carefree bachelor to a responsible husband and father; from an unsure novice to a professional with a sense of vocation; from a parochial Punjabi migrant to an aspiring internationalist with a vision of global peace and harmony that would be realised through service to India, my motherland; and from an erstwhile colonial civil servant to a free spirit keen to explore, experiment and innovate in education. In these two decades, I negotiated thirteen-and-a-half years pursuing an active career, interspersed with six-and-a-half years as a student.

Endnotes

1. The slogan 'Africa for Africans' came to the fore in the wake of the formation of the Kenyan Independence Movement in 1959. Though Asians were initially involved, this movement became mono-racial within months, as historian Sana Aiyar shows. The nationalist emphasis was then on a restoration of rights to Africans as the original inhabitants, and an undoing of the racial hierarchy that placed Europeans on top, Asians in the middle and Africans at the bottom. See Sana Aiyar, 2015. *Indians in Kenya: The Politics of Diaspora*. Cambridge, Mass.: Harvard University Press, especially pp. 229–30.

2. In practice, Africanisation meant replacing European and Asian personnel with African personnel. As Sana Aiyar shows, the Kenyatta government's Africanisation policy led to 33,000 Asians (18 per cent of the Asian population at the time) leaving Kenya in 1967–68, most of them settling in Britain, even as British immigration laws/policies vis-à-vis South Asians were modified as a result. Aiyar's study includes a discussion of the prior role played by trade unionists and leaders like Pio Gama Pinto (assassinated in 1965) and Makhan Singh in the struggle for *Uhuru* (freedom) in Kenya. See Aiyar, *Indians in Kenya*, especially pp. 263–91.

8

USA

1968–72

Late in November 1968, we boarded the S. S. Kampala. It was owned by the British India Steam Navigation Company, one of the oldest colonial shippers of goods and people between Europe, East and South Africa, and India. This was a 29-day sea voyage from Kilindini Harbour, Mombasa to Tilbury Docks in London. It was essentially a holiday cruise, travelling along the east coast of Africa, around the Cape of Good Hope in South Africa and across the eastern Atlantic Ocean. We spent the days sunbathing, swimming and playing deck games. Children, under the watchful eye of trained teachers, played in the well-equipped nursery with paddle pools. In the evenings there were film shows; ballroom dancing and parties were organised on special occasions. The dining hall provided sumptuous meals at breakfast, lunch and dinner. The weather was for the most part sunny and warm, with placid seas. There were three ports of call along the journey. The first was a three-day halt at Durban. We were allowed to go ashore for sightseeing and shopping. Later, the ship laid anchor off Cape Town, but we had to stay on board. At Tenerife, off the Spanish coast, we could again go ashore. Our first experience of the rough seas was during the stretch round the Cape, but really stormy seas were to be seen in the North Atlantic. I came down with sea sickness and could not eat for two days. Sudesh and the children fared better. It was a great relief to move beyond this ordeal by water and to have solid ground under our feet at Tilbury Docks.

Our stay in London with Pushpa, Lakhpat and Deepak was brief, marked by the mix of hospitality, recrimination and blame that seemed to be the pattern of family meetings with them. Three days later we took the flight to New York, paid for by Friends World College, my new employer.

We reached New York on an early afternoon at the end of December 1968, unprepared for the New York winter and still dressed in our light clothing, even though Pushpa had equipped the children with winter wear for the milder English climate. A warm welcome awaited us in the form of Arthur Mayer, director of the North American centre of Friends World College. He had with him warm coats for us all. We put these on and were bundled into a Volkswagen minibus with inner heating, driven by him. Soon we were on our way to Mitchell Gardens on the 12-lane Long Island expressway, whizzing past skyscrapers and across cloverleaf flyovers. We had seen pictures of these wonders of the New World in the movies, but the actual experience of seeing their scale and span in person was stunning.

The Mitchell Gardens campus near Westbury town was an abandoned World War II Air Force base, given on short-term lease to the Friends World College for its global headquarters and North American centre. For a Quaker[1] institution oriented towards world peace, it offered an opportunity to make good the Biblical injunction of beating swords and spears into ploughshares.

The barracks had been converted into offices, student and staff housing, and a dining hall-cum-community centre. They were centrally heated with running cold and hot water. The parade ground became space for a playground. Furnishings for homes and offices were gifted by Friends and neighbours, usually after spring cleaning and refurbishing of their own homes. All the labour for this work was done by students and staff volunteers, with technical support as needed. Salaries were modest and equitable; basic food supplies were purchased in bulk from a cooperative market and provided free of cost. The midday meal was an occasion for the whole community to gather together and began with a common prayer drawn from the scriptures of different faiths. Everyone helped the kitchen staff with work on a voluntary rotational basis. For me, it was a dream come true—a community of kindred spirits seeking meaning, purpose and a way forward through education in a world gone astray in its mindless pursuit of power and pelf.

Our first abode was a long barrack converted into homes for two families. Each had two bedrooms, a kitchen, bathroom and sitting-cum-dining room. Keith and Ellen Helmuth with their children, Eric and Brandon, were our neighbours. They considered themselves 'dropouts' from the 'rat race' to get rich that the average American was programmed into. Keith was a trained technician who had left his factory job to find an opportunity to do meaningful and creative bodily labour, combined with spiritual growth. He had been influenced by the ideas of Henry Thoreau and Hermann Hesse. They had decided not to send their children to school, which according to them was a factory for breaking young spirits and moulding them to fit into the 'System'. They were kind and good neighbours who helped us in every way to settle into our new life. The children easily took to each other and spent most of their time playing games that required cooperation rather than competition. This was a relief for Sudesh, who had to learn to do all the housework herself, without servants. This is where Ellen's help was most valuable: she acted as a role model and guide for us to get used to new electronic gadgetry like the washing machine, refrigerator, vacuum cleaner, mixi-blender, etc. Like other husbands, I helped with dishwashing, bathing the children and weekly cleaning of the house. Very soon, we realised that a car was essential to manage life on

Long Island, since it had little by way of public transport. So Sudesh and I took instructions to get our US driving licenses to enable us to drive a newly purchased secondhand Volkswagen minibus.

Soon after our arrival, I met Morris Mitchell, first President of the college. Morris had been a member of the Koinonia Community in his home state, Georgia.[2] He was a keen advocate of intentional communities and cooperative movements, and saw them as alternative and futurist forms of social relations. He insisted I should make a deeper study of cooperatives, through both literature and experience, to introduce this emerging concept in FWC. To my great regret, I did not heed his advice. As a person and as a public figure, Morris, then in his 80s, was something of a legend amongst people of his generation. He was a farmer and master carpenter who had a work bench in his sitting room. He worked on it daily, making some wooden object—sawing, planing, polishing—while carrying on conversation about education for a better future. He was tall, physically fit and had a ruddy complexion. Even on cold winter days, with the temperature well below freezing, he would walk outdoors in shirtsleeves and a light jacket. He was fond of children, whom he'd take around for walks on campus. In true Quaker fashion, he insisted that everyone, including children, call him Morris without any honorary prefixes or 'sirs'. His wife, Barbara Mitchell, was nearly thirty years younger than him. Barbara was in charge of students' travel. She also arranged group study tours abroad for the general public.

To help me prepare for my academic work, Morris gave me his book, *World Education*, written as a curricular framework for faculty and students. Through it I learnt about the problem-solving approach in education, which was first enunciated by John Dewey, Morris Mitchell's mentor at Columbia University. Morris had elaborated this approach, with an emphasis on discovering and formulating

World Problems and Emerging Concepts as solutions to these problems. Thus war and peace, poverty, environmental damage, nuclear threat, civil and human rights, social and economic injustice, racial segregation, the crisis in education and campus unrest, drug abuse, etc., were seen as World Problems that needed to be addressed. Here, the United Nations had to be treated as a key resource for learning, with planned visits to its headquarters in New York and interactions with the officials and country representatives based there. All this required a structured and pre-planned programme.

Morris introduced the philosophy and plan to the first community meeting of students and faculty. After that, the faculty members spoke about their concerns and the courses they wished to offer. Tony Pearce, Tom Findley, P. Veeravagu, Helen McCormick, Keith Helmuth and Arthur Mayer all had their specialisations but were expected to tailor these into the framework of World Problems and Emerging Concepts. Students were also encouraged to articulate their interests. All this provided the basis for the semester's programme, which was drawn up by the faculty at the beginning of the academic year. The programme had three phases: on-campus orientation, fieldwork experience, and on-campus sharing and journal completion. In the first and last phases, there were weekly tutorials with a faculty advisor for help with planning, expression and self-evaluation. Overall, it was designed as a four-year liberal arts undergraduate programme, with the first semester in the home region, followed by six semesters in other regions, that is, Latin America, Europe, Africa, South Asia and East Asia. Each semester followed the three-phase pattern: orientation, experience and reflection. For the final semester, students returned to the home region to write a senior dissertation on a subject of their own concern and interest.

My academic work initially involved lectures and tutorials on topics of my choice. I focused on the problems of the perceived crisis in education at the time, as well as campus unrest and alternatives in education, drawing on my own studies and current critiques and debates on these subjects. I read and introduced students to the ideas and experiments of John Holt, Jonathan Kozol, Sylvia Ashton-Warner, Paul Goodman and Murray Bookchin. Some of them were invited to speak to students, and we travelled weekly to Murray Bookchin's apartment in New York City to hear him hold forth on anarchism, its concepts and history in Europe.

During the fieldwork phase, I accompanied a group of students on visits to southern states in a Volkswagen minibus. There we stayed with Morris Mitchell on his farm in Georgia. He showed us around his orchards, vegetable gardens and woodlands, which he tended himself despite his age. He also spoke about the need to strengthen local communities. He served us food made with produce from his own garden. From there we headed to the Highlander Centre in Tennessee, founded and led by Myles Horton. He had played a pioneering role in raising awareness and advocating for empowering education amongst poor White and African-American communities in the Appalachian Mountains and the South. These communities had suffered during the Great Depression in the 1930s. He explained to us the methodology of self-expression, role playing and group organisation in the struggle for civil rights and for resisting injustice through non-violence. One of the instances he gave was the case of an African-American woman, Rosa Parks, who, after a spell at the Highlander Centre, refused to give up her seat in the 'White only' section on a racially segregated public bus. She was arrested and charged with breaking the law. This led to massive protests and boycott of buses by African-American workers in Alabama. This episode is, of course, considered

IMAGE 1: Chand Kishore and his brother Prem, London, 1956

IMAGE 2: Chand Kishore (right) with his father Dina Nath, son Tarun and grandfather Behari Lal Sant, September 1973

IMAGE 3: With his wife Sudesh, early 1970s

IMAGE 4: Family photo with Sudesh, their daughter Amita and
son Tarun, 1970s

IMAGE 5: With workers in the rural areas, 1970s

IMAGE 6: With the village community he loved so well, 1980s

IMAGE 7: Walking in village spaces with Udaipur-based Gandhian thinker, educationist and scholar of Mewari, Dayal Chand Soni, 1980s

IMAGE 8: Chand and Prem at Big Ben, 1990s

IMAGE 9: With Sudesh and Tarun at the India International Centre, Delhi, to celebrate the completion of Tarun's Ph.D. in Partition literature, 2006

IMAGE 10: A conversation with distinguished scholar Kapila Vatsyayana at India International Centre after the launch of Tarun's book, *Witnessing Partition*, 2010

IMAGE 11: With grandson Karan, 2012

IMAGE 12: Family photo with daughter Amita, son Tarun, grandson Karan, son-in-law Roopen Arya and Sudesh, 2015

IMAGE 13: With activists Jai Sen and Ashish Kothari at a meeting organised by Shikshantar with Vikalp Sangam, 2017

IMAGE 14: Family photo with Roopen Arya, Sudesh, Amita, Karan and Tarun, 2018

IMAGE 15: Chand Kishore (centre) with dear friends in Goa—Sudesh,
Bina (daughter-in-law of Suresh Amonkar, a friend from the Kenya days),
Tarun, and eminent educationist and scholar of Konkani literature
Suresh Amonkar, shortly before Mr Amonkar's passing in 2019

IMAGE 16: With key Ubeshwar Vikas Mandal personnel, Kesuji Kuria
from Palkhanda and Kesuji from Bagdunda, in recent years

the beginning of the civil rights movement in the 1960s, later led by Martin Luther King Jr.

After visiting some other experimental projects in the area, we reached Washington, DC in time for the historic 1969 Peace March against the Vietnam War, in which over a million people from all over the USA took part. It was a completely peaceful occasion, with everyone in a friendly spirit, singing 'Give Peace a Chance' and 'We Shall Overcome'. For us, it was an exhilarating experience that uplifted our spirits and strengthened our resolve to work for peace and non-violence. On the stage were performances by famous musicians of the era, poetry recitals and speeches by the organisers pledging opposition to the US-led war in Vietnam and calls for a complete withdrawal of troops and negotiations for peace. We never got close to the stage, but it did not matter. The spirit of compassion and goodwill amongst people and yearning for Peace on Earth was abroad and we felt part of it.

After ensuring that each student was settled in their projects, I drove back with the family to New York. This was my first experience of long-distance driving on highways, negotiating the fast-moving traffic, following lane discipline and speed restrictions. We stopped at diners and motels along the way. The nightmarish part was getting across New Jersey and New York City to reach Long Island. Just before entering Long Island Tunnel from New York City, I got into the wrong lane and could not shift in time to take the right exit. I had to carry on into another area before I could do a U-turn and retrace the right way. Eventually, I became quite adept at negotiating the mazes, cloverleaf junctions and flyovers.

During the summer, Barbara Mitchell organised a 'Round-the-World' study tour for the public in collaboration with Pan-American Airlines. It was a package deal, including air travel, top-class hotel accommodation with breakfast and dinner, and local sightseeing. I was invited to be the academic guide. I readily accepted the offer and requested Prem and Raksha to take care of Sudesh and the children in their home in Minneapolis during my absence. There were 15 subscribers, comprising three elderly couples, six middle-aged ladies and three younger women. They were all White and well-to-do.

We all met at JFK International Airport for introductions and briefings before taking the flight to our first stop in Paris. We visited the usual landmarks—Eiffel Tower, Notre Dame church, Arc de Troimphe, the Louvre, the Latin Quarter, etc. In the evening, I gave them some information about the cultural and historical heritage of the city. For this, I drew on my studies and earlier visits to Paris. On the day of our departure, Barbara and I, along with one of the party, went for lunch along Boulevard St Michel. We lingered over the delicious French cuisine, paired with wine, and lost track of time. As a result, we arrived late at the airport and missed the onward flight. The rest of the party was furious with Barbara. It took some effort to calm them down. Another flight was arranged later in the day, bringing us to our next destination, Athens. The warm Mediterranean climate and relaxed atmosphere worked wonders. Everyone became friendly and forgiving of our lapse in Paris.

Barbara and I spent time with them individually and in small groups, getting to know each other better. We did not wish to be their chaperones, but to be with them as companions. Apart from a sightseeing tour of the great monuments of the ancient Greek civilisation, much of the time was spent in outdoor cafes savouring Greek cuisine and being serenaded by street musicians. From here we travelled to Istanbul, where the group was preoccupied with shopping for antiques and carpets to ship home. In Beirut, our favourite pastime was swimming. In Addis Ababa, we attended a briefing by an ex-diplomat on the ancient history and culture of Ethiopia and its present aspirations. From there, we took a flight to Bombay and stayed at the famous Taj Hotel. After two days, we left for Udaipur. I looked forward to this, since I had briefly met Dr Mohan Sinha Mehta, the founder of Vidya Bhavan and Seva Mandir, at Mitchell Gardens. He had come to visit our college and meet its founding trustee, Mary Cushing Niles. In that passing moment he had just said, 'Young man, there is work to do in India'. The words became tattooed in my mind, reminding me of my tryst with Mother India.

On reaching Udaipur, we were taken by bus and then boat to stay at the Lake Palace Hotel in the middle of Pichhola Lake. This is one of the palaces of the Maharanas of the erstwhile kingdom of Mewar, earlier used by them in the summer but now leased to the Taj Group as a luxury hotel. Architecturally, it has the classical touch of the best in Mewar's marble construction and inlay work. A little distance away is Jag Mandir, which was for a year the abode of Prince Khurram (later to become ruler Shah Jahan) who, having unsuccessfully staged a rebellion, fled from his father, the Mughal Emperor Jehangir, and was given refuge by the Mewar ruler. This is where he is said to have got the vision for Taj Mahal, the mausoleum he built for his beloved wife, Mumtaz.

Our purpose in travelling to Udaipur was to visit and see the work of Seva Mandir (SM). This was also my main reason for joining the study tour. When we arrived there we were received by Dr Mohan Sinha Mehta. He briefed us on the idea and work of Seva Mandir. It was inspired by the example of the Servants of India Society, founded by the legendary politician Gopal Krishna Gokhale in Pune in the late nineteenth century. It was conceived as a 'band of workers' with lifelong dedication to service to one's country. Although the idea was put forth in 1931, it did not find concrete expression till 1966, when Dr Mehta retired as Vice-Chancellor of Rajasthan University. He used his savings to build the office and a small residence for himself and was the first 'life worker' of Seva Mandir. Earlier, while serving in Mewar Princely State, he had begun Vidya Bhawan (VB), a progressive school for children that was free of caste discrimination and provided an opportunity for learning and discovery beyond the classroom.

Vidya Bhawan had grown beyond a school to incorporate a teacher training college, handicrafts institute, a basic school and a rural institute, all run by the Vidya Bhawan Society, a self-governing body. For Seva Mandir's early work, Dr Mehta drew upon the services of the Vidya Bhawan staff on a voluntary basis to lead youth and women's activities, work for health and education in slums and organise discussion groups. Seva Mandir's rural work began with an adult literacy project funded by World Literacy of Canada, a philanthropic initiative established by a well-to-do lady appropriately named Welthy Fisher.

The first centre was started in Lakhavali village, 15 km west of Udaipur. That is where we were taken by the project in-charge, Dayal Chand Soni. A literacy class with 20 or so adults was being held on an open-air platform near the village temple. It began with a prayer in Mewari, the local language, invoking Saraswati, goddess of learning, to grant the boon that knowledge may sprout in the hearts of the students. This was followed by reading aloud words written on a blackboard by the local voluntary instructor. The class had been meeting for a few months and was quite competent in recognising basic vocabulary and numerals. Later, members of our group asked questions about agriculture, the food and water situation and healthcare in the village. They were pleasantly surprised to learn that the community was quite self-sufficient for its basic needs. With two assured crops a year, it was able to raise a surplus of maize and wheat for the market.

Our visit to the area ended with a meeting at the office of the Block Development Officer (BDO), sub-district level in-charge of the Community Development Programme. He explained to us the structure and functions of the programme and of Panchayat Raj or local self-government. As I listened, I could sense that it was very much a top-down bureaucratic effort with little regard for people's knowledge and practice, which were considered backward. At one point in the discussion, I wondered aloud why the ordinary village farmers did not feel a sense of responsibility for the quality of life in their own surroundings, on their own doorstep, a lack evidenced by the ubiquitous squalor on the streets. The BDO's response was quite inchoate. In excited tones he defended the efforts of his department, given the shortage of time and resources. He ended with the declaration: 'We have to educate our rulers first. That is our priority in a democratic society.'

Earlier in the village, I had taken the opportunity to talk to people and see their homesteads. It took me back to my childhood days in villages in Punjab, rekindling that special relationship one has with one's place of upbringing.

Back in Udaipur, after the group had returned to the hotel, I talked to Dr Mehta about my desire to return and work in India. He was encouraging and hinted at the possibility of an opportunity to join Seva Mandir. That evening in the village with Dayal Chand Soni and the stay at the Lake Palace left a deep impression and sowed the seeds for a future life in India. While the group departed for Bombay, I took a flight to Delhi for courtesy calls on relatives there.

I rejoined the group in Bombay for the onward flight to Bangkok. After a couple of days of sightseeing and shopping, we travelled to Kyoto via Tokyo. The highlight of our stay there was a visit to the famous Buddhist Toji Temple and Pagoda. There was a deep calm and harmony in the architecture, decorations and environs, especially the grounds with their white-and-grey granite pebbles raked into patterns depicting cosmic waves and whirls and ebbs and flows. Amidst this abode of peace, our group barged in, chatting excitedly about shopping and meals. I tried to calm them down by pointing out the colourful depictions of Buddhist Jatakas and Mandalas on the walls and patterns on the ground, but to no avail. They carried on with their anxieties, carping and commentary about the journey. I decided to walk away to sit and meditate under the carefully tended lone tree in the garden. From then on, I lost interest in communicating with the group and looked forward to the end of the tour, while still helping Barbara with necessary logistic support.

Our last stop was Honolulu in the Hawaii Islands. For some from the west coast, the journey ended in San Francisco. I took the flight to Minneapolis to spend some time with Prem and family before returning to New York with Sudesh and the children. There, utterly exhausted and with an additional day and night in my life's account owing to travelling across time zones, I slept for a week, barely managing to keep awake for bathing and meals.

Back at Mitchell Gardens, I was assigned to lead a course in education with the incoming class. I designed it to include the concepts and history of education systems, the nature of the present crisis and discontents, as well as emerging ideas and experiments. With my background in political geography, I was also asked to assist Tony Pearce, the political scientist, in his course on contemporary world problems. In addition to this, I had to hold tutorials and conduct individual advising with a small self-selected group. There were also duties related to administrative tasks and maintenance of the campus, as well as regular meetings of community, faculty and Board of Trustees. All this was during the first two semesters.

In the third semester in 1969–70, I was asked to lead a group of students for their Latin American Orientation Programme at the Centro Intercultural de Documentación

(CIDOC) in Cuernavaca, Mexico, founded and led by the legendary Jesuit rebel priest, Ivan Illich. Initially, CIDOC was intended to be a Spanish language learning centre for Catholic priests and Peace Corps volunteers from North America preparing for service in Latin America. While continuing this function, it had now grown into a research and documentation facility for critical analysis of the dominant modern systems of health, education, communication, energy, technology, and even Church and charity. The books *Deschooling Society*, *Tools of Conviviality*, *Energy and Equity*, and *Medical Nemesis* were outcomes of this work. The thought dynamo behind these critiques was Ivan Illich partnered with Everett Reimer and with logistic support from Valentina Borremans.

The organisation attracted intellectuals and students from North and South America who, apart from conversations with Illich and others, led seminars on issues of their own concern. Once a week, Illich gave an extempore lecture reflecting his own thinking on research underway at CIDOC. This was the week's most popular event. Occasionally he hosted dinners for selected scholars. We were regular invitees. Over lunch and during breaks, Illich randomly sat for conversations with visitors, interrupted by bites of a chunk of homemade bread. As he used to say, 'No one is unimportant!' While his gaze was gentle as a feather, his comments and questions were sharp as a rapier. He was very fond of children and would often take Tarun and Amita for walks around the campus so that Sudesh could attend some of the lectures.

The students' work began with an initial orientation laying out a broad framework for the semester. The first month was devoted to learning Spanish and planning individual or group projects. This was followed by on-site project work and travel. The last part of the semester was for writing a journal and self-evaluation. My work involved weekly planning and review meetings and individual advisement for their projects and journals. Occasionally, I had to accompany one or more of them to meet potential resource persons and mentors. Since there was no regional centre, I had also to explore the possibility of setting up one in association with CIDOC. This failed because Illich, a product of rigorous European and Ecclesiastic scholarship, had little patience with vague liberal arts studies, which he termed academic tourism. However, we did work out an arrangement whereby students could do Spanish lessons and attend ongoing seminars.

For our personal accommodation, we rented a small furnished villa with a spacious garden and swimming pool, overlooking the town. After breakfast, I walked to CIDOC, which was located atop a hill overlooking the villas. Sudesh and the children would join me there for lunch. In the evenings, we strolled around the town square, listening to the brass band playing Mexican music. Occasionally, we'd stop at small cafes to savour tacos, burritos and other Mexican snacks. For dinner, we usually bought tortillas, which were chapatis made of maize flour on electric machines designed for this purpose. There were special programmes on holidays and festivals, with processions of the Holy Madonna and Jesus Christ the Saviour. On weekly market days, indigenous people in their traditional attire would come with their produce and squat on both sides of the Main Street, knitting woollen shawls. Tarun and Amita had plenty of playmates in the neighbourhood. They picked up the syllables of Spanish, mixed these with English and forged a babble in which they would talk to each other. We could not follow this and worried whether this would impair their speech and language learning later. At bedtime, we talked and read to them in English without any problem. Thus, it seemed they had developed a kind of bilingual facility of their own. All this vanished once they were back in New York.

At the end of the semester, students returned to Cuernavaca to complete journals and evaluations. For most of them, it had been a fulfilling experience to be on their own in a country with a different culture and language. They had adjusted well and had a lot to express in their journals. For some, however, it was difficult. They felt they had not received adequate faculty and peer support. This was understandable since this was also my first experience of its kind and I had to learn on the job. But all this was in keeping with the nature of the FWC educational experiment.

Back in the North American campus, we spent summer vacations partly at home and partly in upstate New York, attending the annual conference of the New York State Meeting of The Society of Friends or Quakers, the founding and proprietary body of FWC. This was held in their sprawling holiday facility on the shores of one of the smaller lakes. It had family accommodation, a common dining hall and a conference centre. There was a well-organised programme of meeting for worship, business meetings, caucuses, committee work and general assemblies with invited speakers. For each of these, there was a clerk of the meeting who prepared minutes that were read out at the end for consensus. One of the important features of the conference was the reports of local meetings and of special committees for service, education, peace, race relations, gender and the environment. There was a special committee for FWC. One of its members, James Holden, who was a trustee of FWC, presented the report. This received both appreciation for the visionary venture and criticism for its vagueness and lack of intellectual rigour in its programme.

The beginning of the new academic year in September 1970 saw some major changes in FWC. Morris Mitchell retired as president. Reny Hill, as vice-president, stepped in to lead the administration. A search committee was set up to find a new president. Sidney Harman, a businessman with acumen in electronics, joined the Board with a promise to improve FWC's financial situation. Later in the year, he took over as President. Barrington Dunbar, specialist in

Black Studies, joined the faculty, as did Surinder Suri, a political scientist with Marxist leanings. There was student unrest around several issues—the size of administrative staff, campus facilities, fees, curriculum, state of overseas centres, lack of counselling for students with special problems. There were endless community meetings where students poured out their grievances. One day it all erupted in a poster protest, with posters plastered across the walls of the dining hall showing vulgar, abusive sketches of staff. Some of us immediately took the posters down before breakfast.

A community meeting was called to share our concerns and thoughts about this occurrence and the atmosphere on campus. We realised that student discontent with the academic programme, oversized administration, food and students' representation had to be addressed. A working group comprising staff and a student representative was formed. I was asked to join. Wide-ranging consultations were held with students, faculty, administration and trustees and written submissions were also invited. There were significant differences between the students' expectations and faculty preferences, as well as among faculty. Most of the students wanted a more flexible curriculum with freedom to design their own study programme. The older faculty wanted some component of the curriculum to be devoted to serious academic work, while others were prepared to put their faith in students' self-designed experiential learning, supplemented with appropriate readings suggested by faculty. Some staff and trustees wished to hold on to the original World Education framework.

After several meetings, the working group proposed the following for consensus:

- Maintain World Problems/Emerging Concepts as a framework rather than a foundation course;
- Include courses designed by faculty as additional options;

- Accept the principle of a programme with students' self-designed study/experience/project for all centres;
- Streamline and minimise administration, giving students opportunities to take responsibility in this area;
- Retain the component of study abroad but with flexible schedules, strengthened centres, special opportunities to non-American students and improvements in the resource database;
- Maintain a regime of low tuition fees, with simple living and self-help.

This was approved and adopted with some modifications by the community, faculty and Board of Trustees.

As mentioned earlier, during the 1970–71 session, Dr Surinder Suri, along with his wife Donna, joined FWC. He had studied and worked in India and had a PhD in international relations from Northwestern University. We became good friends. He had a good collection of books on India, which he shared generously. Surinder helped me to deepen and update my knowledge of India. He also noticed a negative trait in my attitude towards others, a sort of animus for those who crossed me in arguments and disagreed with my views, and advised me to correct it. There were some ferocious stray dogs on campus, perhaps the progeny of canines trained for guard duty at the erstwhile airbase. They regarded the college as an infringement on their domain. Most of us avoided them, but Surinder and Donna befriended them and would walk fearlessly in and out of campus with the dogs as escorts!

Surinder introduced me to *Seminar* magazine and I became a regular reader. On one of my visits to India as Coordinator of Independent Study, I visited the *Seminar* office in Delhi and met Romesh and Raj Thapar. I shared with Romesh my work with FWC and with Ivan Illich at CIDOC in Mexico. He was keenly interested and encouraged me to plan an issue of *Seminar* on Alternatives in Education.

I wrote a brief statement of problem and did an interview with Illich. The issue came out perhaps in 1971 or 1972. Eventually, when I decided to return to India in 1972, I had long conversations with Surinder Suri about the problems and situation in India and my aspiration to work there on Gandhian lines. He wrote to Romesh about this. Later, he showed me Romesh's pithy reply, with the phrase 'neo-Gandhi?' I took it as an endorsement of my decision to return and a sign of Romesh's regard—and perhaps yearning—for the Mahatma, despite his own Leftist inclinations.

The second visit to CIDOC in Mexico was in the third semester of the academic year, 1970–71. Owing to my earlier experience, I was able to manage it with more confidence. After orientation and settling students in their projects, I was able to engage more substantially in CIDOC's activities. This took two forms. One, I anchored a weekly seminar on Gandhi, based on Erik Eriksson's book, *Gandhi's Truth*. It began with my presentation to visiting scholars on the scope of the seminar in the weekly *El Ciclo*, published by CIDOC. After that, 25 students and others signed up for the seminar. There were reading assignments for each session, based on which a discussion was initiated. My role was to provide the historical and cultural context for exploring Gandhi's concepts of God as Truth, Satyagraha or insistence on truth, ahimsa or non-violence, Swaraj or self-rule and their practical application in life. One of the salient ideas in the book is Eriksson's definition of Gandhi as 'Homo Religiosus'. In his words:

> …while he [Gandhi] learned to utilise craftily what was his first professional identity, namely, that of a barrister English style, and while he then became a powerful politician Indian style, he also strove to grasp the 'business' of religious men, namely, to keep his eyes trained upon the all-embracing circumstance that each of us exists with a unique consciousness and a responsibility of his own which makes him at the same time zero and everything, a centre of absolute silence,

and the vortex of apocalyptic participation. A man
who looks through the historical parade of empires
and civilizations, styles, and isms which provide most
of us with a glorious and yet miserably fragile sense
of immortal identity, defined status, and collective
grandeur, faces the central truth of our nothingness—
and, mirabile dictu, gains power from it.[3]

Based on this concept, I prepared a brief note as my contribution to the ongoing seminar at CIDOC on 'Alternatives in Education'. Illich appreciated it and marked it for publication in *El Ciclo*. In addition to all this, I interviewed Illich for *Seminar* Magazine, as mentioned earlier.

Before leaving Mexico, we visited St Miguel de Allende, Oaxaca, Chiapas and Acapulco. This gave us glimpses into the country's rich history and culture through the centuries, ranging from the pre-Columbus Mayan civilisation at Oaxaca, to the living traditions of tribal life in Chiapas, to the meticulously conserved Spanish town of St Miguel de Allende and finally, to the modern seaside resort town of Acapulco. In Mexico City, we visited an art gallery which exhibited the paintings of Diego Rivera.

Back at Mitchell Gardens, there were major changes in administration during 1970–71. Sidney Harman took over as president. We had got to know each other during Board meetings and had developed a kind of rapport. He was impressed by my ideas of self-designed learning and independent studies. He appointed me Coordinator of Independent Studies and, after Arthur Mayer's retirement, to the post of Acting Director, North American Centre. These major responsibilities involved endless community, staff, faculty and Board meetings, and frequent travel to overseas centres for development and troubleshooting. Sidney treated me as his confidant and academic advisor, taking me along in his sports car to important New York State Board of Regents hearings on education and on the status of the FWC. During these journeys on the Long Island expressway, we had long conversations on the problems of education, mostly in terms of my responses to Sidney's questions.

After the move from Mitchell Gardens to Lloyd Harbour, Sidney often visited us at our new home in Northport to play table tennis with me and entertain the children with his sleight of hand tricks. He confided to me that as an expert in electronics, he had played a key role in decoding enemy messages during World War II. After the war, he set up a business manufacturing high-fidelity music systems under the brand of Harman Kardon. This became famous around the world much before Sony and other Japanese versions. As music lovers, we purchased one of these at discounted rates to enjoy Indian and Western classical music.

Sidney's stint as college president did not last long. At Board meetings, he made elaborate presentations on budgets and cash flows, but his plans to improve the financial situation of the college did not yield tangible results. There were heated debates about his style of functioning and doubts about his understanding of and commitment to the educational mission of Quakers and the FWC. Mary Cushing Niles, one of the founding trustees and a practising Quaker, took a personal dislike to Sidney. He was made to resign. To save face and lend a radical touch to his decision, Sidney declared that he would continue his association with the college as a student. During this somewhat unpleasant episode in the politics of the college, as a faculty representative on the Board I had to make some difficult choices. On the one hand, Sidney had recognised my capacities for innovation and creative resolution of differences and given me the opportunity for leadership. We had also developed a personal compatibility regarding our distinct but complementary roles. On the other hand, there was the larger aspect of his relationship with the Board, whose trust he had lost. In the end, I had to set aside my personal considerations and go along with the Board's position. Later, Sidney completed his doctoral work with University without Walls, expanded his business and rose in the political ranks to the post of Under-Secretary for Commerce in the Jimmy Carter administration. We kept in touch and on one occasion that I shall later recount, I had reason to visit him.

Sidney's departure once again created a crisis of leadership. There were prolonged discussions amongst the students, faculty, staff and Board. Various options were explored. Robin Hodgkinson, student representative on the Board, wanted FWC to become a leaderless, self-managed community without a president, while more conservative trustees were in favour of the status quo. Ultimately, a compromise was reached and it was decided that the college should be headed by a Troika comprising of one member each from the faculty, student and administrators. The first Troika was formed with Reny Hill (administrator), Robin Hodgkinson (student) and Kishore Saint (faculty). In those revolutionary times of student unrest and campus revolts, this novel arrangement evoked interest in academia and the larger public. It received coverage through reports in *The New York Times* and *Long Island Post*. My presence in the Troika as a person of Indian origin was noticed by a community paper, *India Abroad*, in far-away California.

In mid-1971, FWC shifted to its new campus at Lloyd Harbour, further east on Long Island, a spacious, picturesque waterfront estate gifted by a friend of the college. Rented accommodation was arranged for us in Northport, a few kilometres east. The house belonged to a German lady who herself lived in another house some distance away. She helped Sudesh to settle in and showed her the facilities for shopping in Northport and Huntington, the main urban centre nearby. The children were admitted to nursery school in Northport.

Since they had to be driven to school, another car had to be purchased. Sometimes a system of carpooling was arranged with neighbours for this purpose.

Soon our life settled into a routine of driving to work and school, taking the children to the nearby park to play, followed by Baskin-Robbins ice cream and then home for TV and supper, bath, bedtime reading and tucking the children in to bed. For bedtime reading, we used Dr Seuss's readers, which featured illustrations and were designed to facilitate letter and word recognition while listening to the stories. This enabled Tarun and Amita to read at the ages of five and four years, respectively. Weekends were given over to housekeeping, shopping and, occasionally, picnics and parties with the children. Sometimes I was invited to give talks to local community groups. At one of these, I spoke on Tolstoy's interpretation of Christ's teachings on non-violence and their relevance in our strife-ridden times. Coming from a Hindu, this was well appreciated.

My work in the College involved more meetings and consultations on policy and management. The Troika now had Janet Walker, a senior, as student representative and Jim Truex as administrator.

Since independent self-designed learning was an important part of the FWC experience, I prepared a working paper on this, drawing upon the key ideas of learning developed by psychologist Carl Rogers. As he puts it in his book *Freedom to Learn*,

> I dare to believe that when the human being is inwardly free to choose whatever he deeply values, he tends to value those objects, experiences and goals which contribute to his own survival, growth and development, and to the survival and development of others. I hypothesise that it is characteristic of the human organism to prefer such actualising and socialised goals when he is exposed to a growth-promoting climate.[4]

As a moderator of the Troika, I had to make trips to centres abroad for policy sharing, planning, problem-solving and generating new ideas for the future. At the European Centre in Cambridge, England, I met two faculty members, Richard Lannoy and Victor Clark. Richard was the author of *The Speaking Tree*, a rich cultural depiction of India based on his travels and conversations with scholars, holy men and women, and people from different walks of life. I shared with him and Violet, his wife, my plans to return to India. They were excited to hear this. Violet was interested in exploring work in teacher education with Vidya Bhavan. After dinner, we listened to Ravi Shankar playing various *raga*s on the sitar. This sent Richard into a trance; he was shaking his head, tossing about his long, flowing hair and beard. I could not meet any students as they were away on their projects.

The centre in Kenya in the small market town of Machakos often had problems in communication between the Kenyan director, Ezekial Kagode, and American students. Here the consultant, Sheldon Weeks, had to act as a mediator.

The India Centre in Bangalore was set up through the personal efforts of Mary Cushing Niles. As a Quaker, she was deeply involved with Indian spirituality. She was a devotee of Rehana Tyabji, a Muslim mystic and a follower of Gandhi, whom she visited without fail on her visits to India. With her personal contacts in high places, she was able to overcome the suspicions of the bureaucracy about FWC being another US Central Intelligence Agency (CIA) front. The centre was headed by N. Krishnaswamy, with G. Sampath as administrator and E. P. Menon as faculty. Later, Surinder Suri joined as a faculty member.

Since I had indicated to the Board my decision to return to India, the search for a new moderator of the Troika had begun. It eventually focused on George Watson, a political science professor who was about to retire from the University of Chicago. He and his wife, Elizabeth, were devout Quakers.

They came to meet me both before and after accepting the job at FWC. We had long conversations on my understanding of FWC's mission and how it functioned. Elizabeth was an admirer of India and of Hindu philosophy; she had studied the writings of Gandhi and Tagore. George went on to work with the college for fifteen years. After his retirement in the mid-1980s, he and Elizabeth came to India on what they called a pilgrimage of Gandhi's ashrams and Tagore's Santiniketan. They visited us in Udaipur. That is when we got a glimpse of Elizabeth's spiritual depth and George's serene wisdom. We also shared with them the ideas and scope of my work with tribal communities and Sudesh's work with children through the Hans Open School. Later, Elizabeth wrote *Guests of my Life*, a book based on their experiences, and sent us a copy.

In early 1971, I became part of an Indian study group on poverty, motivated by the slogan of 'Garibi Hatao' ('Eliminate Poverty') given by India's Prime Minister at the time, Indira Gandhi. It was anchored and hosted by a research scholar from Kerala. We met weekly at his flat in Manhattan, where each of us took turns to present our views on the nature of poverty. I drafted a note for one of the meetings, taking the discussion beyond economics and into institutional and cognitive domains.

The last function I attended as the moderator of the FWC Troika was the commencement ceremony for graduating students in May 1972. This was held under a marquee on the lawns of the Lloyd Harbour campus. Mary Cushing Niles, Board chairperson at the time, had invited U Thant, former Secretary-General of the United Nations. I had to give a welcome address with a brief report on the progress of the college. In this, I stressed the path-breaking role of the college within the field of education, and in addressing the problems of world peace, injustice and environmental degradation. I highlighted the role of students as survivors in the early phase of this experiment and as pioneers in the self-designed cross-cultural learning underway at present. I concluded by acknowledging the importance of the United Nations as an inspiration and resource in this venture, and hence the appropriateness of U Thant's presence at the event. U Thant, in his address, commended the New York Yearly Meeting of the Society of Friends for their commitment to world peace and for putting into practice the visionary idea of world education for this purpose. He also openly criticised the US involvement in the war in Vietnam. After the ceremony, Janet Walker and I had the opportunity to chat with U Thant. The event was publicised in *The Long Island Press*, which featured a photograph of the three of us in its report.

After this, most of our time was taken up with packing and shipping our belongings to India. On our journey back to India, we stopped over in England and Kenya for FWC work, holidays and for the purpose of meeting relations and friends. In Kenya, Bharati Vasudeva, husband of Raksha's sister Sneh, gave me his red sports car to drive to Mombasa.

On reaching India, I had to make a visit to Bangalore to sort out problems at the FWC Centre there. Our next destination was Vidya Bhawan in Udaipur.

ENDNOTES

1. 'Quaker' is a colloquial term for the Religious Society of Friends, a set of Christian denominations that emerged in the mid-seventeenth century. Members of this religious movement are referred to as 'Friends', or sometimes as 'Quakers'.

2. 'The Koinonia community, named for the Greek word for fellowship, was established on a farm in Georgia in 1942, based on the principles of the early Christian church. Resources were to be pooled and all persons regarded as equals, regardless of their racial background.' See Chancey, Andrew. 'Koinonia Farm'. *New Georgia Encyclopedia*, last modified 8 June 2022. Available at https://www.georgiaencyclopedia.org/articles/arts-culture/koinonia-farm/ (accessed 13 June 2023).

3. Erikson, Erik H. 1969. *Gandhi's Truth: On the Origins of Militant Non-Violence*: 396–97. New York: W. W. Norton.

4. Rogers, Carl. 1969. *Freedom to Learn: A View of What Education Might Become*: 254. Columbus: C. E. Merill Publishers.

9
Return to India
1972–75

We left New York at the end of May 1972 and reached Udaipur in early July on a flight from Bombay. On arrival, we were met by a Sardarji who, without introducing himself, picked up our luggage and asked us to follow him. We thought he was a porter. Once outside, he put the luggage in a car and asked us to get in. 'I am here to take you to Vidya Bhawan,' he said. Still we saw him as a taxi driver or a driver employed by the institute. It was when he began to talk to the children in fluent English that we discovered he was Baljit Malik, the principal of Vidya Bhawan School. He took us to his home, a double-storey, three-bedroom bungalow set amidst spacious grounds. He told us that this was where we'd be staying as his guests. This would be our home for the next seven years, shared for one year with Baljit, after which it would be ours alone. Baljit was from Delhi, the scion of a Punjabi Sikh family of wealthy building contractors who had built some parts of Lutyens' Delhi, the centre of the planned British imperial capital. He had studied history at St Stephen's College and had earlier taught at his alma mater, the Doon School. Baljit was a generous host. We learnt that he had married an English woman, but they had separated. He had a black Labrador, Impy, who slept in his room.

After a day or two to settle down, we met other colleagues at Seva Mandir, among them Kamla Bhasin, Om and Ginny Shrivastava, Chhaganji Mastersab, Ram Krishna Sharma, Dadabhai K. L. Bordia and K. N. Shrivastava, all involved in leading different institutions and activities. Eventually I met the founder and *Adhishthata*, Dr Mohan Sinha Mehta, to discuss my specific responsibilities. Before arriving there, I had understood that I'd be involved in some leadership capacity in the teacher education work of Vidya Bhawan (VB). But to my surprise, Dr Mehta suggested I take up the directorship of the Vidya Bhawan Rural Institute (VBRI). Apparently, this had to do with the internal politics and hierarchies of VB. Backed by other senior trustees of VB, K. N. Shrivastava, the director of VBRI at the time, had to be promoted to the post of principal of the Teacher's College, the senior-most paid position in the organisation. So I was asked to take his place at VBRI. I had no option but to accept, since we had not considered any other job possibility and there was no question of returning to Friends World College. However, I did feel trapped and let down. From my earlier visit in 1969, I had understood Vidya Bhawan and Seva Mandir's work as being carried on in selfless service for the upliftment of Indian society. In our correspondence before coming to Udaipur, I had conveyed to Dr Mehta that joining him in his educational work was, for me, in the spirit of a *yagya*, a sacred, sacrificial engagement in which the first *aahuti* (offering) was oneself. This was the ideal I had held before me. But now I was face to face with this institutional reality. Reconciling to this situation, I tried to give it a virtuous spin: *majboori ka naam* Gandhi, so to say! I remembered my own upbringing in villages, the *Gurukul* where I had spent a year as a child, and the prize I had won for lauding village life over city life. Gandhi's dream of 'Gram swaraj' and Vinoba's Bhoodan–Gramdan movement also came to mind.

Properly settling down in 'Putliwala Ghar'—as our new abode, Vidya Bhawan Guesthouse, was known as—involved many adjustments, especially for Sudesh and the children. Sudesh had to go to Bombay to receive the luggage we had shipped by sea. For this, a bribe had to be paid to officials. A two-tiered bed was made for Tarun and Amita. A sofa set was also bought for the sitting room and a low, octagonal table of stone, set in an iron frame, was made for us to dine on while seated on the floor. For transport, we depended on Baljit's car for six months, till our Bajaj scooter was delivered. This was on priority basis since we had arranged the payment in dollars. Soon Baljit moved to a staff flat in the VB hostel. We had to engage a new helper for cooking, cleaning, etc. The children joined the VB Montessori School and soon picked up Hindi. Sudesh was engaged with VB and taught English to the senior classes.

In October 1972, an invitation came to 'Bhaisab', Dr Mehta, to a national conference on Basic Education at Sevagram, to be inaugurated by Prime Minister Indira Gandhi. He asked me to attend on his behalf. The journey there took 36 hours by train. I found myself in the same compartment as Janardan Rai Nagar or 'Jannubhai', the Vice-Chancellor of Rajasthan Vidyapeeth, the other major educational institution in Udaipur and in some ways a rival of Vidya Bhawan. He had been a teacher at Vidya Bhawan and was widely recognised as a Hindi scholar and writer with a special interest in Adi Shankaracharya. At any time he was a forbidding presence, as I was to discover later. Being cooped up with him in a sleeper cubicle was overwhelming. He was meticulously dressed in a khadi dhoti, kurta and jacket. Jannubhai liked to talk. Throughout the journey, he assailed me with stories of his association with Vidya Bhawan and with the history of Dr Mehta's family. In particular, he recounted the exile of one of Bhaisab's ancestors from Udaipur Darbaar and the family's reinstatement with the grant of a *haveli* outside the city walls. He also dwelt on the more progressive outlook of Vidyapeeth, with an emphasis on workers and rural education, in contrast to Vidya Bhawan, which catered to the middle class.

I cannot recollect much of the happenings at the conference. Indira Gandhi came for the inauguration. Alighting from the car, she walked briskly to Bapu Kutir to pay her respects to the Mahatma. She made a brief speech with her usual intensity, stressing the need for commitment to the values of national unity and secularism. She left soon afterwards to meet Vinoba Bhave at Paunar Ashram before flying back to Delhi. For the rest of the inauguration, there were opening speeches by some of the stalwarts of Nai Taleem ('Basic Education'), like Manubhai Pancholi of Sanosara Vidyapeeth in Gujarat, who reiterated the spirit and principles of education for the purpose of 'Sarvodaya' and 'Swaraj'. These were followed by an address by Union Education Minister, Nur-ul-Hassan, outlining government policy and plans for scientific education. After the inauguration and a sumptuous lunch, top political dignitaries left the conference, letting the officials, Basic Education workers and academics get on with routine deliberations.

The event was an example of the government policy of periodic consultation with field-based workers even as they carried on with the established system of education. It was also a political exercise—the 'Congress system' of providing patronage to constructive work organisations.

For my work at VBRI, I made a careful study of the K. L. Shrimali Committee Report, which had spelt out the original scheme of rural institutes. The core idea had been taken from the model of land-grant colleges in the USA, with their three-fold function of teaching, research and extension for the economic, social and cultural improvement of rural communities through education. For this purpose, generous funds were provided to acquire land for agriculture, housing for teaching staff and students, and for administration. In the USA, with its flourishing tradition of local democracy, these colleges were under community control. In India, their management was entrusted to voluntary organisations like

Vidya Bhawan. Flush with funds, the institute acquired a large area of cultivated land adjacent to the Chikalwas feeder canal in the 1950s.

Vidya Bhawan Rural Institute was one of a dozen or so institutions set up to train personnel for the Community Development Programme of the Government of India, in tandem with the launch of the Panchayati Raj scheme for local self-government in rural areas. During the 1960s, India had faced major crises due to drought, wars and the failure of rural development, resulting in food shortages and near-famine conditions in some areas. In response, emphasis was placed on agricultural development using high-yielding varieties (HYV) of seeds and chemical fertilisers as part of the Green Revolution. This was accompanied by the setting up of agricultural universities and downgrading of rural institutes. When I took over at VBRI, it had all but given up on its original purposes, becoming a low-grade degree college academically and closing down its extension work in villages.

The three-year stint at VBRI was perhaps the most trying and challenging assignment in my career. It was a situation rife with institutional politics where the appointment of an outsider as director was bitterly resented by senior academic staff. There was intense rivalry for control between academic and administrative staff. Trustees too had their favourites. My appointment was a compromise and in deference to the wishes of Adhishthata, the founder-president. I had no inkling of this, nor any preparation for the cauldron of intrigue and power play I was thrown into and where I had to provide leadership.

I soon discovered that the person really in command was Sunder Lal Vyas, the Executive Secretary, overall in-charge of administration and finance. For these functions, he had built up his own loyal team of workers. At lunch break, they all sat together and reviewed the state of affairs in the institution. I'd join them to get a feel of the situation. The teaching staff had their own cliques, under the overall leadership of four senior teachers who, at the time, were unhappy with the central management of Vidya Bhawan and the excessive power of the executive secretary. The engineering section was self-contained and run efficiently by its own principal. In addition, there was some residual research and extension staff, an agricultural advisor and a farm manager. There was also a defunct carpentry production-cum-training centre. The farm provided training in improved agriculture to farmers from surrounding villages, who worked there on a seasonal basis.

My office was in the administration block. I decided to work on an open access basis where anyone could knock on the door and meet me. As word got around, staff and senior students came to meet me individually. I encouraged them to share their views on the state of affairs in the institute. They were not always candid or objective, but did convey a picture of the different interests at work and tensions amongst them. Some of them would pour out their own grievances and injustice suffered. I tried to understand their position on the founding principle of VBRI as an organisation providing education for rural community development. Only a few in agriculture extension and administration believed in its validity and the need to hold on to this goal. Others saw no future in it, especially for students, as rural studies did not lead to job opportunities. The department of civil engineering, however, was different. It was run as a well-disciplined unit under the leadership of C. S. L. Agarwal, an experienced and loyal hand with a good grasp of Vidya Bhawan dynamics and of the profession.

In these conversations I could not fathom the truth and wrote these lines:

> *Satya kya hai? Chhupa hua hai, iss meethi muskaan ke peechhe...*
> *Satya kya hai? Daba hua hai shabdon ke toofan ke neeche*

*Satya kya hai? Khel raha hai moocchhon ke iss taanv ke
bheetar
Satya kya hai? Ghuta hua hai aahon ke sunsaan ke andar…*

(What is truth? It is hidden behind that sweet smile…
What is truth? It is drowned under a storm of words
What is truth? It plays behind that arrogant moustache
What is truth? It is stifled within a desolate sigh…)

Since VBRI, as a degree college, was affiliated to Udaipur University, it had to follow curricula and faculty standards approved by the academic council of the university. Some of the senior faculty found out about my qualifications, and through their contacts, the university raised the question of whether my Master of Education degree was equivalent to the Master of Arts degree, the minimum requirement for a faculty appointment. The matter was referred to the University of Birmingham, who clarified that as an academic and research qualification, their M. Ed. was indeed equivalent to a Masters in Arts. I attended one or two academic council meetings and could sense the hostility amongst some of the members, who resented that someone with foreign qualifications had been appointed to a senior position. The animus of VBRI senior faculty also came out in the weekly Saturday assembly, whenever they were given an opportunity to speak. There were also reports of faculty with affiliations to political parties inciting students against the management and director.

In these adverse circumstances, I decided to leave the academic and administrative staff to their own devices, performing only the formalities of signing routine documents and notices. Instead, I turned my attention to the extension function and revived the defunct Yuvak Mandals in the rural service area of VBRI. The Yuvak Mandals had been active earlier and were meant to involve the village youth in voluntary activities for the all-round improvement of life in their communities. With the help of agriculture advisor Devaki

Vallabh Sharma and farm manager Kanhaiya Lal Bapna, key village youth leaders were identified and a leadership training camp arranged. I personally took responsibility for this and stayed with the group for five days at a time in a village.

The programme followed the ashram pattern, based on the idea of self-help. We followed a routine of rising early, attending morning prayer and briefing, breakfast, physical labour (*Shramdan*) to build or repair a community asset, followed by a bath and lunch, sessions for talks and discussion, afternoon rest, games, supper and then sleep. On some evenings, local Bhajan Mandalis were invited to sing devotional songs. They had a wide range, from Kabir, to Raidas, to Meerabai and Chatursinghji Baasab. These sessions often lasted the whole night, concluding with early morning *Prabhati*. Despite this, there was no sign of fatigue and the next day's programme continued as usual. I found it difficult to keep awake all night and had to excuse myself to get some sleep.

Duties were assigned on a voluntary basis for the preparation and serving of meals, cleanliness and other tasks. Since the participants had different caste backgrounds, some of them were reluctant to partake of the food prepared and served by others. The matter was discussed and a principle laid down—that caste-based discrimination was not acceptable and those who could not abide by this should leave the camp.

Most of the discussions were led by me. I tried to re-evoke the idea and spirit of the village community and stressed the importance of Yuvak Mandals in setting an example and providing leadership in promoting social education, agricultural improvement, village sanitation and civic responsibility. I coined the phrase '*Vikas Aaj ka Yug Dharma Hai*' ('Development is the Imperative for this Age') to convey the importance of development. For technical aspects, specialists were invited from an agricultural university and government departments. Dr Mehta took a keen interest in these initiatives and would personally spend a day at the camp. After this leadership training, similar camps were arranged in all 25 villages in the VBRI service area. These were appreciated by the local officials and panchayat representatives in the area, who gave the initiative their full support.

After a few months, I decided to assess the impact of these trainings at the village level. This was done through community meetings in selected villages. These were well-attended, but there was a reluctance to speak up. The leaders tried to present a glowing picture of the Mandals' activities. However, it soon became clear that the reality was very different. There were no regular meetings or self-initiated community effort. Only literacy classes run by workers trained at the Seva Mandir were held regularly. Although intended for adults, they were attended mostly by children and youth who were dropouts or had not gone to school.

With the launch of the Green Revolution, there were active campaigns for the introduction of HYV seeds and chemical fertilisers in agriculture, led by farmers' cooperatives, the agriculture department of the government and the agricultural university in the state. For this, farmers with larger landholdings and irrigation facilities were selected and provided training, generous subsidies given for inputs, along with assured markets for their produce, mostly maize and wheat. The successful demonstration of new technology and the benefits it brought had a widespread impact on farmers. A whole new ethos of production for the market and an enterprise based on self-interest was introduced in the countryside. A prevalent slogan was, '*Tum Apna Vikas Karo, Samaj ka Vikas Apne aap Hoga*', that is, you develop yourself and society will take care of its own development. This contributed to undermining the traditional kinship, caste and village-based community duties and obligations.

It was also contrary to the ethos of community development that rural institutes were supposed to promote.

In each village, there were individuals who saw outside institutional contacts as an opportunity to promote themselves. There were also others, usually elders, who still valued the sanctity of community, nature and divinity and tried to restrain the incursion of new-fangled ideas. I tried to maintain a balanced approach between the two, but the relentless pressures of political leaders, bureaucracy and markets, combined with the severe drought distress and shortages in 1972, made the adoption of new technologies and involvement in their institutions inevitable. Even so, Yuvak Mandals, through voluntary labour, were able to create or repair community assets like school buildings, playgrounds, the village pond and the common well.

In some cases, larger projects like road construction were undertaken as drought relief work, in collaboration with Seva Mandir, under the 'Food for Work' Programmes supported by international agencies. Payments for work were made in the form of foodgrains (wheat or maize) donated by foreign governments, notably the USA and Germany. For livestock, free fodder was distributed. This was brought by truck from Punjab, Haryana and UP.

Drought distress was particularly acute in hilly tribal villages with poor road access. I visited some of these in the Dhar–Ubeshwar area with the help of my driver, Ambalal Gameti. This was my first exposure to the Bhil tribal communities, people whose plight, culture and environment would become my major interest and preoccupation in the years to come. At the institute's annual sports day, I arranged a special event for these villagers, a mini-marathon race starting from Dhar and ending at VBRI. Twenty or so took part, traversing a distance of 15 kilometres over hilly terrain in under three hours. The winner was Uday Lal Gameti of Banadia.

At VBRI, I also tried to revive the spirit of voluntary work by starting campus cleaning and kitchen gardening with staff participation. Only a few of the administration, extension and research colleagues came forward, while the teaching staff openly mocked the effort as a gimmick, as demeaning and as backward-looking. Students too kept their distance. Among trustees and management, there was bemused tolerance.

An interesting feature of Vidya Bhawan was the inter-institutional common assemblies and celebrations. Every Saturday morning, the school, teachers' college students and staff gathered on the school lawn, which was surrounded by stately trees. The assembly began with the singing of VB's own prayer, '*Antartam Mein Jyoti Bharo Hey*....' ('Fill the darkness inside me with Light...'). This was followed by reading passages from the writings of savants and sages. Once in a while, visiting dignitaries addressed the assembly. Republic Day and Independence Day were celebrated by flag hoisting and speeches by the President and heads of institutions. 21 July was observed as Foundation Day at Sajjangarh Fort-Palace. Everyone walked the 12-kilometre hilly track. There were cultural performances by students and *kachori*s and *jalebi*s were served. Bhaisab, as the founder, Adhishthata and patriarch of Vidya Bhawan, which he regarded as his family, distinct from his kinship connections, presided over these functions.

One of the reasons for our move to India was to enable Father to live with us. Accordingly, he emigrated from Kenya and joined us in March 1973. He soon settled into his routine, keeping his asthma under control during summer months. Some of the Vidya Bhawan staff would drop in and spend hours listening to his wisdom, poetry, memories. Word also got around about his being a Theosophist. The Udaipur lodge of the Theosophical Society invited him for talks on different religions and on spirituality. The president, Mr Hydari, personally took Father in his car to these meetings. Our grandfather, whom we called Bhaiyaji, came to spend some time with us. He stayed in the same room as Father for three weeks. During this time, they were closeted for long hours, talking to each other, sharing their memories, joys, sorrows and remorse, and trying to reconcile with each other.

After the drought in 1972, the monsoons were at a record high in 1973. This aggravated father's asthma and he became bedridden. After Bhaiyaji left, his condition worsened and he had to be hospitalised. There he passed away on the night of 18–19 September. I was with him at the time. The funeral was attended by workers of Vidya Bhawan, Seva Mandir, Udaipur University and other educational institutions, signifying the sense of community that prevailed in the voluntary sector at that time. Last rites were performed on the banks of the Ayad River, which was in flow. I informed Prem over the telephone. Bhaiyaji and other relations were informed by telegram. He, Shanti Bhuaji, Srinivas Phuphadji and Rameshwar Chacha came for the fourteenth-day ceremony, which was performed with a simple Arya Samaj *havan* conducted by a local priest. As was the custom, I was expected to shave my hair and beard. I politely declined the suggestion. Perhaps this was due to my vanity and assertion of individuality. Prem came in December, when we both went to Haridwar to immerse Father's ashes in the Ganga. Later, many friends and well-wishers sent messages of condolence and appreciation for Father's many qualities and his spirit of service.

Along with my work at VBRI, I took on responsibilities in Seva Mandir on a voluntary basis as secretary and convenor, Sanchalak Mandal or Directors' Council, for the planning and coordination of different activities. These included the Discussion Group, Mahila Mandal, Dramatics Society, Youth Club and Students' Forum. The Dramatics Society, under the leadership of Kamla Bhasin, staged three plays—Vijay Tendulkar's *Khamosh! Adalat Jari Hai*; Mohan Rakesh's *Aashaad ka Ek Din*; and Girish Karnad's *Hayvadan*.

Khamosh! was directed by Shail Choyal, a well-known artist. The other plays were directed by Bhanu Bharti from the National School of Drama. I played the role of Ponkshe in *Khamosh! Adaalat Jaari Hai*, while Amita was part of the cast of *Hayvadan*.

Kamla was also in charge of drought relief work, of which well-digging and deepening was an important part. Identification of new well sites was often undertaken with the help of local water diviners. The exception was an Englishman, Mr Davenport, manager of the Lake Palace Hotel. On one occasion, I accompanied him and Kamla to find a location for a new well in a nearby village. It was around dusk. As we walked across the dry fields, the double-forked stick in Mr Davenport's hands began to reverberate as if it were energised. He walked to and fro till the pointed end of the stick bent down at one spot. 'This is where digging should start,' he declared and walked away, visibly shaken by the experience. As luck would have it, water was found there. But this was not always the case with him or other local diviners. Eventually, agencies and the people themselves brought in trained hydrogeologists with their technology, while still relying on traditional diviners.

In the summer of 1973, our friend and trustee of FWC, Mary Cushing Niles, visited us. Her purpose was to persuade me to return to Friends World College. She did not make it explicit, but felt my talents were being wasted in Udaipur, 'a one horse town'. I did not give much thought to the matter as I had resolved that India was not only my *janmabhoomi* (birthplace) but it had also to be my *karmabhoomi* (the place of my life's work), the *Kurukshetra* where I had to find my life's purpose, my destiny. Mary Cushing left disappointed, but we stayed in touch. In 1977, she invited me to New York for a three-day global consultation on the future of FWC.

Bhaisab's career as a diplomat and as Vice-Chancellor of Rajasthan University had given him wide-ranging contacts at the national and international level. He was on various advisory bodies as chair or as a member. Among these were Indian and Rajasthan Adult Education Associations. These were forums of non-government voluntary organisations set up by concerned citizens devoted to specific causes, and their membership included both non-officials and officials. They held seminars and conferences in different locations hosted by member organisations. These gatherings had a festive and friendly atmosphere that promoted a sense of comradeship and common cause. I accompanied Bhaisab to these events and got to know important persons, whose support we could draw upon for local work.

Among them was Anil Bordia, an alumnus and scion of the Vidya Bhawan family, by then an Indian Administrative Service (IAS) officer with a special interest in education. He was impressed by my background and thinking. He'd consult me on matters of policy and involved me as member in the National Adult Education Programme Advisory Board and in the Central Board of Secondary Education. In the former capacity, I contributed to the writing of a handbook for adult education teachers. This was done in a three-week workshop at the Indian Institute of Education, Pune, under the guidance of legendary scholar and social scientist J. P. Naik. Ivan Illich visited India at the invitation of ICSSR. I met him in Pune.

Through these wider engagements, I began to develop a perspective on social change in post-independence India, with a special focus on Gandhian values, voluntarism and voluntary organisations. I discussed this with Ranjit Gupta, an economist. He had been an associate of Sarvodaya leader Jayaprakash Narayan (JP) and was now working with Ford Foundation. They had asked him to organise a conference on the role of voluntary agencies in rural development. Ranjit asked me to prepare a keynote paper for this, which I presented at the conference held in Hyderabad. Following this, a national-level group, The Association of Voluntary Agencies in Rural Development (AVARD), was set up with JP as its patron. Later, I served on its executive committee.

Through these activities, I also came in contact with major Gandhian organisations like the Gandhi Peace Foundation, Gandhi Smarak Nidhi and Sarva Seva Sangh. I started attending their annual *Sammelan*s (gatherings), where I met the older stalwarts of the Gandhian movement, notably Dada Dharamadhikari, Acharya Ramamurthy, Vimala Thakkar, Govindrao Deshpande, Thakurdas Bang, Sidhhraj Dhadda and Radhakrishna. Author Ved Mehta had designated them as Gandhi's apostles in his book, *Gandhi and His Apostles* (1977). Geoffrey Ostergaard, political sociologist and my host in Birmingham, described them as non-violent revolutionaries. They were all approachable and I was able to discuss with them my concerns about voluntary movements.

Some of them were active in the pre-Emergency era JP movement, when differences arose amongst them about their position regarding the policies of Prime Minister Indira Gandhi. Vinoba Bhave, Gandhi's spiritual heir, did not favour the agitation launched by Jayaprakash Narayan against the PM. As a result of these differences, there was a split in the Gandhian movement. On one occasion I accompanied a group of JP supporters to meet Vinoba Bhave and pose some questions to him. It was the day on which he observed silence, so his response was given as written notes. Egged on by others, I rather rudely asked Vinoba about the reason for his failure to openly criticise the illegalities being committed by the regime. This annoyed him and he wrote back a peevish reply. I countered it with '*Kya ye aaj ke yug ki sant vaani hai*?' ('Is this the voice of a saint of this age?') He wrote back with 'Jai Hari!' and closed the conversation. Vinoba, as an ascetic-activist, was an advocate of subtle non-violence (*saumya ahimsa, satyagraha*), in which the essence/force is the purity of spirit or intention with which an act is performed. Later, I realised and regretted my foolhardiness in confronting a self-realised and revered figure like Vinoba.

In the course of Seva Mandir's drought relief work, I came in contact with international agencies like OXFAM, United Nations Food and Agriculture Organization (FAO) and Youth against Famine, Action for Food Production (AFPRO), and the 'Freedom from Hunger' campaigns supported by them. In 1975, I attended a major policy consultation on poverty alleviation organised by OXFAM at the Social Work and Research Centre at Tilonia, set up by Sanjit 'Bunker' Roy and Aruna Roy. There, in the presence of OXFAM chairman Brian Walker and other top executives, I presented a paper on the role of voluntary agencies in the present, 'frankly apocalyptic' context of progress and its impact on nature. It evoked only mild amusement at my quaint English usage. Despite the 1972 Stockholm Conference on the environment, ecological issues were not on the agenda of most charities in the 1970s. Poverty was their main concern—at Stockholm, Indira Gandhi had termed it 'the biggest polluter'. Beyond provisions for relief in times of crisis, development was considered the panacea for poverty alleviation.

An exception to this view was Colonel B. L. Verma, a retired army engineer who was working with Action for Food Production. He was concerned about increasing water shortages and traditional methods of water usage and conservation. As an example, he cited the Chittorgarh hilltop fort-palace with its elaborate system of rainwater drainage and storage in tanks. This had enabled the inhabitants to survive months of siege during wars. Later, in collaboration with AFPRO, water conservation became a major concern and programme for Seva Mandir.

During Prem's visit in December 1973, a meeting of academics, professionals and officials was organised at Seva

Mandir to raise concerns about environment issues. It was chaired by Bhaisab. After the meeting, a committee was set up to address the problem with Dr T. P. Jain, principal of RNT Medical College, as its convener. Soon afterward, Dr Jain was transferred from Udaipur and the committee and its concerns about the environment remained unrealised.

Visiting Sevagram after seven years, I was able to spend some quiet hours taking in the atmosphere and spirit of the place that had witnessed momentous and historic events like Gandhi's fast against separate electorates for Harijans. It was also the venue of experiments in constructive work, like Basic Education, the Swadeshi movement, gram swaraj, care of cows, composting, biogas and, above all, a training centre for satyagraha. During my three-day stay, I tried to follow the ashram routine of early morning and evening prayers, physical labour for cleaning activities and help with serving meals. Later, as I became more involved with Gandhian organisations, I visited Sevagram frequently for meetings and conferences of the Sarva Seva Sangh and Sarvodaya Samaj.

Another memorable visit was to a conference at Banwasi Seva Ashram in Mirzapur district of UP, set up by the activist couple Prembhai and his wife Dr Ragini to serve the tribal community in that remote, densely forested area. They started by providing relief in times of distress. Inspired by Gandhian principles, they were trying to evolve a Swadeshi model of development through the use of local materials and skills for housing, food, healthcare and education. Participants had been invited from voluntary organisations across the country to see this approach and to discuss policy and direction for voluntary work in India.

The conference was held under the aegis of AVARD, supported by a German Catholic charity, Misereor. Its consultant in India, Badal Sen Gupta, was present, as were some executive committee members of the association. Over five days, issues related to poverty in India were discussed and policy and experiences reviewed. The conference concluded that the approach so far had been top-down, creating dependence. It needed to be more participatory, involving the community and relying on their organisations and capabilities, supported by voluntary agencies as catalysts. For me, it was an opportunity to learn about the state of the voluntary sector in rural development in India and make contacts for resources for Seva Mandir's work. At the same time, I had a glimpse of the decay that had set in within older institutions like the Gandhian Institute of Studies in Varanasi. On our way to Banwasi Seva Ashram, we had to stay there in a hall for a night. The place was full of litter and dust. There was no one to clean it. As everyone stood around, I picked up a broom and started sweeping. Some others joined in and soon the room was made liveable for the night.

On the way back, a local participant took me around Varanasi for sightseeing. This was when I had the opportunity to meet the legendary Thumri singer Girija Devi at her modest home in a lane within the old city.

Back in Udaipur, after the severe drought of 1972, the monsoon in 1973 was record-breaking, with 51 inches or over 1,200 mm of rain. As a result, all the lakes overflowed, there was water-logging and even flooding along the Ayad River. At one point the flood water rose to a height of 6 feet at the Siphon road junction outside the VBRI gate. Some students trying to wade through were caught in the current and had to be rescued with the help of strong swimmers and a sturdy rope. I personally oversaw the operation.

At Seva Mandir, an important occasion was the inauguration of the Seva Mandir library by Pandit Hriday Nath Kunzru. He was a member of the Servants of India Society, founded by the statesman and scholar Gopal Krishna Gokhale, who had mentored Gandhi in his early political career. The Society and Gokhale had inspired Bhaisab to set up similar initiatives in Udaipur through his Rangers troop in the field of scouting. This troop undertook a trek to Pindari Glacier in the Himalayas in the early 1930s, during which the idea of Vidya Bhawan crystallised. The Seva Mandir library foundation was laid soon after, but it took over four decades to complete the building. The inauguration was a simple affair, with the traditional lighting of lamps on a brazier. I was invited to light one of these, signalling a recognition of the leadership role I was expected to play in Seva Mandir.

Among other important visitors there was Shri Jagdish Chandra Mathur, a retired officer of the Indian Civil Service (ICS), the precursor of the IAS, the powerful and privileged steel frame of bureaucracy through which the British had ruled India. During our conversation, Shri Mathur told me that on the eve of India's independence, top civil servants such as himself were ready to shed their perks and move to modest living arrangements. But it did not happen due to Nehru's preferences and the general aspirations for higher standards of living, modelled on the lifestyle of colonial masters.

Towards 1974, in the politically charged pre-Emergency atmosphere, senior teachers disgruntled with Bhaisab and Vidya Bhawan management instigated the students to agitate against me. There were frequent demonstrations with sloganeering. On one occasion they tried to prevent my entry from the main gate of VBRI. As I stood outside, one of the administration staff, Vishnu Gaur, confronted the students and insisted on my entry, and opened the gate. A few of the students kept shouting, but others kept their distance and did not interfere as I walked in. Apparently, they did not have any conviction in what they had been put up to do. Soon after, a section of the teaching staff decided to prevent my functioning as director. A message was sent around, threatening my disrobing if I came to office. The matter was discussed with Bhaisab, who advised that I, along with my family, should leave Udaipur for a while. Early next morning, Baljit took us in his car and put us on a bus for Ahmedabad.

We stayed there for a few days with Kamla Bhasin's brother, K. K. Bhasin, and his family. He was then aide-de-camp (ADC) to the Governor of Gujarat.

Although necessary for the safety of the family in those circumstances, running away from that challenge was a humiliating and cowardly experience. It reinforced my disenchantment with VBRI. On our return, I asked Bhaisab to relieve me from my responsibility. He personally came to the office and took over the charge from me. Thus ended three years of a futile effort to revive a failed institution of higher studies and community education for rural development. However, the experience gave me a grounding in the rural reality in Mewar. It also reconnected me with the traditional, ancestral past in which I had grown up. It was a process of self-recovery as well as the basis of a renewed relationship with a sense of purpose and responsibility. Over the next three decades, these village communities would become my *karmakshetra* and *dharmakshetra*.

While I was personally able to find direction, for Sudesh it was an ordeal to move from a caring, well-provided, egalitarian, progressive and orderly community in the USA to a parochial, faction- and caste-ridden situation with undercurrents of both resentment and fascination towards outsiders. Since I had to travel a lot, she had to bear the burden of looking after both the children and Father and managing the household. Further, she also taught English to senior classes in Vidya Bhawan. Baljit Malik, Kamla Bhasin and her sister Bina, nicknamed 'Guddi', and Sardar Arjun Singh's wife were the Punjabi group who provided support to make her feel at home.

An important aspect of the adjustment in our new phase of life in India was Tarun and Amita's education. As educators, we knew about the various approaches and options, ranging from home education to Gandhian Basic Education, to English-medium day and residential public schools. As it happened, all these except Basic Education were explored. To begin with, both Tarun and Amita joined the VB Montessori school in the Upper Nursery class with Margaret, 'Gabo', a young Australian teacher. They adapted well to the free and open play atmosphere with special Montessori learning toys. Miss Amarjit Kaur, an affectionate Punjabi Sikh teacher, taught them Hindi. After the first year, Amita continued in VB, while Tarun was admitted to St Paul's, an English-medium school run by Catholic priests. He lasted exactly two days in that school. Put off by corporal punishment, he refused to go to any school. We had no choice but to take responsibility for his education at home. We bought self-instruction books in English grammar and mathematics that were suitable for his age. He accompanied me to VBRI, where I gave him guidance.

Along with this, since both of them had an interest in reading and could read well, they borrowed books from Vidya Bhawan School and Rural Institute libraries to read on their own. Tarun, at the age of nine, read V. S. Naipaul's classic, *A House for Mr Biswas*. During one of my visits to Bangalore, I met the author and mentioned this to him. He was somewhat mystified and perhaps offended, since the book was not meant to be a children's novel. Later, Amita and Tarun saved their pocket money to buy Enid Blyton books, which had begun to reach Udaipur. Of course, there was also a good collection of fiction at home that they could draw upon. Apart from studies, there were opportunities for friendships and play with children in the neighbourhood. Amita was more open to these, while Tarun only went out in the evenings to play cricket with boys in our front yard.

Our cultural interests in art, music and theatre brought us in contact with the artist families of Shail Choyal, Maand singer Maangibai and Ghazal singer Prem Bhandari. We arranged music evenings at home and in Seva Mandir. Amita began learning Bharatnatyam with Rajamani, the dance teacher at Vidya Bhawan. He told me about Kalakshetra, the dance academy set up by Rukmini Arundale, the celebrated Bharatnatyam dancer. I went to see it during one of my visits to Madras and was impressed by the atmosphere and devotion to the ancient dance form. We gave serious thought to sending Amita there for training. However, Sudesh was unwilling to let Amita go so far away from home. Tarun made a start with learning to play the *tabla*, but did not continue.

We celebrated the festivals of Makar Sankranthi, Basant Panchami, Shivratri, Holi, Baisakhi, Diwali and Sharad Purnima in accordance with local customs and traditions, which were still vibrant and centred around family, neighbourhood and community.

For instance, Holi was celebrated with performances of the folk dance *Gher* in every neighbourhood for a full month before and after the day of the festival. *Holika ropan*, or the planting of a pole from the *Semal* (silk cotton) tree, was done at the beginning of the month of Phagun, according to the lunar calendar. *Holika dahan*,[1] marked by setting fire to a stack of farmyard waste, was done on a full moon night in a common gathering. The size and shape of the blaze was considered an indicator of the nature of the next monsoon— plentiful or scarce. Newborns were taken around the blaze for blessings. Popcorn and *rewari* (sesame seed and jaggery balls) were offered into the blaze and distributed as *prasad*. After the blaze died down, only the *semal* pole, which symbolised Prahlad, was left unburnt. The next morning, on Dulandi, Holi was played with the smearing and splattering of colours, singing, dancing, eating, drinking and making merry. After the celebrations, good wishes for the year ahead were exchanged.

The festival of Holi has a special association with Krishna Bhakti. It is the occasion of *Maharasa*, the cosmic love dance of Krishna with the Gopikas. Krishna temples are colourfully decorated and idols of the god adorned with special makeup.

The Shrinathji temple in Nathdwara and Jagdish Mandir in Udaipur are the major sites of celebrations.

Today's writing of my memoirs has coincided with the festival of Shivratri, the night of Shiva. For Mewar, the festival holds special significance. The royal family of the erstwhile kingdom of Mewar traces its origin to Bapa Rawal, a cowherd, to whom Eklingji, a Shivalinga, was revealed at Kailashpuri, 18 km north of Udaipur. They consider Eklingji the real ruler of Mewar and themselves as His *dewan*s or trustees. The complex of temples is located in a side valley off the main road that passes through the major gorge. Many devotees from Udaipur and surrounding areas make a pilgrimage on foot to Eklingji on this day. The *garbhagraha* or sanctum sanctorum gates are opened for *darshan* (worship) at fixed times during the day and *rudraabhishek*, ritual cleansing with cow's milk followed by the dressing of the idol, is performed. People fast for the day and all-night *jagran* or vigils are held, where devotional songs are sung by Bhajan mandalis. In the coming years, I would discover the deeper ecological significance of the worship of Shiva and his consort Parvati or Gauri in the lives and legends of rural communities, especially Bhil tribals.

ENDNOTES

1. The ritual fire on Holi symbolises the mythic episode of Prahlad. Prahlad was the son of the king Hiranyakashyap and was punished by the king for his faith in the Hindu god, Vishnu. The young boy was forced to sit in a blazing fire, but miraculously emerged unscathed.

10

Seva Mandir

1975–83

The year 1975, when I shifted from Vidya Bhawan Rural Institute to full-time work as development secretary at Seva Mandir, was marked by other changes in the institution and in the country. Kamla and Baljit got married and shifted to Delhi. Later, Kamla took up a job with the United Nations Freedom from Hunger Campaign and moved to Bangkok. Adult education work was under the charge of Om and Ginny Shrivastava. My main interest and responsibility remained rural development.

In June of that year, a state of internal Emergency was declared by the government and many leaders and activists involved in Jayaprakash Narayan's youth movement against corruption and for total revolution were arrested.

My initial response to the Emergency was a sense of relief that order had been restored to what had become a chaotic situation, with agitations and indiscipline all around. It was only later that I realised the restrictions of freedoms and curbing of constitutional rights that it entailed. Bhaisab was more sanguine. As a liberal, he was unhappy that this had happened, but he kept his opinion to himself. As a retired diplomat and educationist, he enjoyed considerable respect and status. He had also kept his distance from party politics. As a result, he and the institutions he was associated with remained free from the harassment and excesses that were committed elsewhere. In general, there was no protest against the Emergency in Udaipur. However, well-known Gandhian

Deen Dayal Dashottar, along with his wife Sushila Dashottar, held a symbolic protest by marching to Ghantaghar with a poster. They were stopped by the police and escorted back to their home.

Some of the young people in Rajasthan who were associated with radical leftist and JP movements sought refuge in voluntary organisations. Bhaisab, a liberal in thought and inclination and radical at heart, gave them space and protection in Seva Mandir. We involved them in adult education and rural development projects. However, along with these initiatives, some of them carried on with their own radical propaganda and organisation within communities. It was rumoured that some, as followers of Mao Zedong, even had guns in their possession. During a field visit, I confronted one of the young men with the question of whether love or hatred should be the force for change in society. As a believer in historically ordained class enmity and conflict, he maintained that class hatred was the necessary motive force for change. This forthright expression was unusual as these young people were generally secretive and kept their views to themselves. On a one-to-one basis, I could engage them in argument, but there was never any collective deliberation on ideological differences amongst Seva Mandir workers, which ranged from extreme left to liberal to Gandhian. After the Emergency, most of them left Seva Mandir to pursue professional or political careers.

I had become involved in adult education during Om and Ginny's absence from Seva Mandir for further studies in Canada. Anil Bordia, an alumnus of Vidya Bhawan and son of Dadabhai K. L. Bordia, had joined the Indian Administrative Service and was then joint secretary in-charge of adult education in the union government. He was leading the recently launched National Adult Education Programme (NAEP), and was a believer in the key role of field-based voluntary agencies in this programme and had great respect for Bhaisab personally, as well as for his contribution to adult education. He asked me to join the NAEP as a member of its working group. In this capacity, I took part in shaping the policy and approach of the programme, taking it beyond adult literacy to create social and civic awareness and improve functionality in livelihood-related work. In order to create 'awareness', I brought in the ideas of Brazilian educator-philosopher Paulo Freire, articulated in his book *Pedagogy of the Oppressed* (1970). He had invented a method of literacy instruction through which key words could be used to create critical consciousness and a greater understanding of their life situation amongst the poor, which would act as a means of their empowerment. This proved too radical for NAEP and was not accepted, but the basic tripod framework of literacy, functionality and awareness was adopted.

To prepare new material for training personnel in this perspective, a workshop was organised at the Indian Institute of Education, Pune, founded by the scholars J. P. Naik and Chitra Naik. I spent three weeks there, working with specialists. My focus was on the training of frontline adult education instructors at the village/neighbourhood level. A subgroup was formed to prepare a handbook for these instructors. I was made convenor. While planning the handbook, I found that other members were not prepared to think beyond literacy instruction. So I decided to work alone on drafting it and submitted the manuscript before the end of the workshop.

Another project that I became involved in at Anil Bordia's behest was training coordinators for the newly launched Nehru Yuvak Kendra's (NYK) programme, run by the central ministry of education. NYKs were set up as district-level centres to support Yuvak Mandals or youth clubs in villages. Here, my experience with the training of leaders in these groups at VBRI became valuable. I organised NYK coordinators' training along the same camp pattern as I had done for the Yuvak

Mandals, involving self-help, physical labour and the sharing of experiences. On one occasion, coordinators from Punjab refused to clean their own utensils after eating, considering it below their status as government officers. I confronted them and insisted they follow camp discipline or leave the training. The matter was also discussed in a general session, where I explained the rationale and importance of setting an example to bring about changes for the better. Impressed with this work, Anil Bordia proposed setting up a full-fledged training facility for NYK at Seva Mandir under my leadership. This was discussed with Bhaisab, who favoured the idea because it would bring in much-needed resources. However, I did not agree, fearing this would tie Seva Mandir too closely to government control and dilute its autonomy as a voluntary organisation. Since the proposal hinged on my leadership, it was not pursued. My fears proved justified when later we learnt about the development of a resource centre for the Rajasthan Adult Education Association in Jaipur, which was made an extension of the state bureaucracy.

Some other short-term projects that I was asked to organise were a week-long study programme for visiting American students and a sociological survey of rural households for the Life Insurance Corporation of India. The latter was done in collaboration with the late Dr Shambhu Lal Doshi, professor of sociology at the University of Udaipur. With a team of students, he organised the survey fieldwork and data analysis while I provided overall guidance and wrote the report. One of our conclusions was that the concept of life insurance had to be broadened in the rural context as the lives of people were closely integrated with their livelihoods, based on agriculture, animal husbandry and forestry. Therefore, life insurance had to be tied to crop and animal insurance. This was problematic for the sponsors of the research.

During my time in VBRI, my driver, Ambalal Gameti, had introduced me to young people and elders in Dhar–Badanga villages, located in a valley at the foot of the ridge leading to Ubeshwar Mahadev Shiva temple (Shiva was considered the protector of that area). We had travelled in a jeep on a rough track running along the Ubeshwar Nala. The people I met belonged to the Bhil community, the main tribal group of western India. In a large community gathering that took place subsequently, the young leaders told me that their main problem was the lack of all-weather road access to Udaipur as the track became impassable during the rainy season. They also talked about distress due to droughts and the need for relief in the form of work, food and fodder. This too was worsened by lack of proper access to the area. Interestingly, there was a difference of opinion about the need for a motorable road. While the young favoured it, the elders felt that it would interfere with their traditional way of life and lead to greater harassment by forest officials and police. Much of the area had been declared reserved and protected forest land under the control of the forest department. After long deliberation, the decision was taken to construct an all-weather road. Seva Mandir was approached for help. The work was sanctioned under a Food for Work project in which wages were to be paid in the form of wheat donated by Germany.

Before starting work, an auspicious day and time were selected for *Mahurat*, when sacred rituals of offerings, prayers and worship to seek forgiveness and blessings were performed. This was done in the presence of the Panchayat Samiti Pradhan, Kishen Trivedi, a Brahmin who doubled as purohit or priest. The final act of the ritual was the tying of sacred thread on the wrists of everyone present to pledge support to the project as a sacred duty, and to indicate its sanctity as a community effort. I too was included in this. It evoked in me a sense of duty and responsibility for the task and marked the beginning of a long relationship with the place and people. The sacred thread remained on our wrists till our work was completed.

After the return of Om and Ginny Shrivastava from Canada, I lessened my involvement in adult education and gave more time to rural development. Here, the experience of recent recurrent droughts led us to undertake water conservation as a major activity. This took the form of a small watershed development project involving soil conservation, reforestation, pasture protection and building of water reservoirs. This project was undertaken in Kherwara Block with the support of Action for Food Production, AFPRO, a voluntary agency. It was the first of its kind and would become the seed model for later watershed development work undertaken by many agencies in the hilly drylands of western India. Initially, it was conceived as a technical intervention for soil and water conservation and to provide irrigation to small farmers. Later, it also included a component of community participation in planning as well as some contribution to costs in execution. Another initiative was the Lab to Land Project, which introduced high-yielding varieties of maize and wheat to small and marginal farmers, along with irrigation facilities.

In due course of time, different components and approaches were combined into projects for integrated rural development, community education for rural development and peer group projects. In addition to adult education and agricultural improvements were included the promotion of cottage industries, training for the maintenance and repairs of new farming machinery, and the construction of biogas plants. An organisational structure based on using village clusters to locate Seva Mandir support staff was adopted. Each cluster team had workers with social, educational and technical skills.

In 1978, I had the opportunity to visit Thailand and Vietnam as a part of a group of educators to study the educational systems in these countries. The group was led by Dr Chitra Naik, Director, Indian Institute of Education, Pune, and included officials and non-officials involved in adult education. They were selected by Anil Bordia, who was by then secretary in the Ministry of Education, Government of India. Our study tour was organised and hosted by the Governments of Thailand and Vietnam. It involved observing programmes and interacting with adult educators. Our group met every evening to review and share our experience and questions. I tried to raise issues about our approach in adult education in the light of our observations, but these were disallowed by Dr Naik, who insisted on giving her interpretation of what we were exposed to. For me, some of the memorable moments from this tour included meeting Vietnam's Minister of Education in his humble abode on a street in Hanoi, seeing the street artists with their watercolour landscapes and visiting a crafts market with traditional pottery in Ho Chi Minh City (formerly Saigon). I bought a set of these paintings and a large flower vase. We were also impressed by the quality of early childhood education and the generous resources provided for it in Thailand. In Vietnam, adult education work was carried on by Party cadres in times of both war and peace. Even soldiers on active combat duty continued their learning and teaching in barracks and in the field.

Seva Mandir in the 1970s was a place of internal experiments, deepening community engagement and broadening external contacts. Various approaches were tried in adult education and rural development, with an increasing emphasis on people's participation and decentralisation of responsibility. Since many of the projects' staff members came from rural areas around Udaipur, the idea of Seva Mandir serving as a training ground and resource facility that could enable these workers to undertake education and development in their own rural communities began to be discussed. To set an example for this approach, I took the initiative to construct a small office-cum-residence in Dhar village. Another centre was built in Kaya village, south of

Udaipur. In other areas, rural centres were set up in rented premises. Workers were encouraged to spend as much time as needed in the field, interacting with people, understanding their needs and planning with them. I provided the lead in this by staying overnight in rural centres for meetings and devotional singing sessions.

While this hectic project activity went on, there were within me undercurrents of discontent and doubts about the adequacy of Seva Mandir's work in the face of the massive drought distress caused by the deforestation of the region. A series of events precipitated a personal crisis, culminating in my decision to leave Seva Mandir.

During the drought distress of the late 1970s, I encouraged workers to be more active in urging local representatives and officials to provide relief for affected communities. A young Rajput field worker in Kherwada confronted a sarpanch, head of the local body, in this matter. The sarpanch, also a Rajput, annoyed at this affront, slapped the worker. On hearing this, I immediately rushed to the village and called a meeting of people to discuss the incident. I felt that the sarpanch's highhandedness should not be ignored and proposed a sit-in by the people at the sarpanch's house till he apologised. Meanwhile, Om Shrivastava, secretary in charge of the area, arrived with a police official. He was not in favour of direct action by the people and left it to the police to settle the matter amicably. I refrained from contradicting him. However, the incident brought out the difference in our approaches to the worker–people–authorities dynamic.

Another occasion was the annual conference of the Rajasthan Adult Education Association, organised at Officers' Training Centre Udaipur. As drought distress deepened, I suggested to the people in Dhar area that they gather at the conference venue and express their plight to delegates. A couple of hundred villagers came over and stood at the main gate. I requested the organisers to give some of them an opportunity to speak. This was declined. As I stood with the people explaining this, local Congress party leaders appeared and started reprimanding the villagers for daring to come on their own with their grievances. One of them pointed to the gold earrings worn by one of the villagers and said, 'You should be grateful to Congress for bringing you to this condition of prosperity.' No one spoke back to him. I toyed with the idea of suggesting to conference organisers that they at least provide the people with a meal, but decided against it and advised them to disperse. As luck would have it, soon after, dark clouds covered the sky. There was heavy rain, good enough to prepare for sowing the winter crop. At least the Great Spirit did not remain indifferent. It responded where human agency failed to do so.

In 1981 I was appointed as Chief Executive Office (CEO) of Seva Mandir. Over the year after my appointment, I made an earnest effort to build consensus amongst the president, secretaries and financial advisor, Shri Mehtab Chand Mehta, around the core values of service to the people, eschewing power politics and factionalism. I attempted to build mutual trust and inculcate a sense of crisis regarding the plight of people and the environment, with a spirit of sacrifice and reasonable parity in remuneration. This was done through a series of monthly meetings. The desired objective was not achieved as there was a lack of openness and no willingness to face the truth and the differences.

Meanwhile, another drought in 1982–83, combined with a lack of adequate relief work, brought deep distress amongst tribal Bhil villages, forcing them to survive by cutting down the remaining forests. The growing lines of head loaders carrying firewood and charcoal began to loom large in my consciousness. I shared this with Dr Mehta. He took note of them during his morning walks along Fatehsagar and tried to talk to the head loaders about the damage they were doing to their future. They told him they had no alternative but this to feed their families. Dr Mehta may have shared his concern with the government, but there was no response. Colleagues in SM and other voluntary organisations too were not overly concerned. I met the Collector and shared with him my anguish, but he pleaded helplessness due to a lack of funds.

All this led to a unilateral decision on my part to stage a symbolic, peaceful sit-in or dharna and fast on the pavement in front of the Collectorate, together with tribal villagers from Dhar, in early January 1983. I conveyed this to Dr Mehta, who remained noncommittal. Some of the other workers were in favour of this plan and came to help. Most kept their distance. Sudesh joined me during the day. An awning and screens were hired to protect us from the cold at night. When Sudesh went to get a ground sheet from Seva Mandir, Om Shrivastava refused to give it to her, saying that the dharna was not an institutional decision. She brought one from Hans Open School, the experimental school that she was running at the time, on our scooter. In the evening, Dr Mehta came to see me. Although he did not support my action, he showed some understanding about my decision. That night passed peacefully, with some of the villagers staying with me. The next day, after making a petition to the Collector for adequate relief, we decided to end our demonstration. The action received some notice in the local press. In Seva Mandir, opinion was divided. Only a few felt it was justified. Most considered it not in accord with the institution's policy, which might even have been placed in jeopardy. In hindsight, I realise it should not have been undertaken without consultations with the workers.

For me, the experience initiated an inner churning as to my being and role in Seva Mandir. I spent more time in the field, particularly in Dhar area, talking to people, listening to their woes and observing how they survived severe water, food and fodder shortages. In this, I was accompanied by a group of young men from the area. I advised them to think about coming forward and taking responsibility to deal with the situation, rather than depending on outside organisations. The upshot of these discussions was that they should form their own organisation, with members from the four villages in what was locally known as Dhar Patti. A meeting was arranged at the newly built Seva Mandir Dhar Centre on 26 January, celebrated as Republic Day. I explained to them the idea of a republic and democracy as government by, for and of the people, and how this could be applied at the village level in the form of village republics. A unanimous decision was taken to form the 'Ubeshwar Vikas Mandal', named after the local deity Ubeshwar Mahadev. This was sanctified by an all-night vigil and bhajan singing. It ended at dawn by singing *Prabhati*. I came away feeling fortified by the collective will and resolve of that group of young Adivasis to bond together to deal with the immediate drought crisis and for the future betterment of their area and people. I also felt that at this juncture, this was where my *karmabhoomi* lay in terms of making my contribution to my country.

After that experience, I began to lose interest in the work of Seva Mandir and increasingly felt out of place in the organisation. Sometime in late February 1983 I submitted my resignation to the president, Dr Mehta. He was taken aback. He wrote to me to say that the resignation was not a wise move on my part and that I should rethink my decision. In any case, he said it would have to be placed before the Board of Trustees. A meeting was called. Some questions were raised about why I had decided to leave. I explained that I wished to work directly with people in need and in a more active manner than was possible in Seva Mandir. Knowing about the dharna earlier in the year, one of the trustees, an ex-bureaucrat, remarked that I would most likely end up in jail. To my surprise, Dr Mehta asked when I was planning to leave Udaipur. I told him I had no such plans. My resignation was accepted, allowing me to leave Seva Mandir at the end of May.

In order to announce the decision to the rest of the Seva Mandir workers, a general meeting was called. Dr Mehta made the announcement. Then he added a personal note. He felt that my decision to sacrifice my relationship with Seva Mandir for the sake of a cause was a cruel step on my part. He compared this to Turkish leader Kemal Ataturk's willingness to sacrifice companions for the sake of his beliefs. I heard it all in silence. When asked whether I wished to say something, I told the gathering it was entirely my own decision to leave; I had no complaints and wished Seva Mandir well. No one else spoke either for or against the decision. Later, in the 1983 annual report of Seva Mandir, my resignation was mentioned by Dr Mehta.

Over the next three months, preparations had to be made to find a new place to stay. One of my colleagues at VBRI, farm manager Kanhaiya Lal Bapna, now retired, offered us accommodation in his old house, not far from Seva Mandir. It was an old-style house constructed entirely using stone, and comprising three bedrooms, a lounge, an inner courtyard and a large compound. There was enough space for our residence and for Hans Open School. We shifted there in May, together with the school. Without my salary from Seva Mandir, we managed with our savings and my pension from government service in Kenya, but the bulk of the income came from Sudesh's salary as principal of the open school. This enabled us to support Tarun and Amita, who were both at private boarding schools.

Earlier, during the 1970s, there had been several developments and adjustments to be made in family affairs. Sudesh and the children visited the UK in 1976 to spend some time with Sudesh's family there. On their return, her mother came with her to live with us for a while. In 1977,

Tarun, then 11, got admitted to Mayo College in Ajmer. It was not easy for him or for us to send him away from home at such a young age. But it had to be done for the sake of his education, as there were no suitable opportunities for him in Udaipur. Amita, after a couple of years in Vidya Bhawan School, joined St Mary's School for a while, but could not adjust to convent school discipline. Meanwhile, Sudesh also took up teaching English in Vidya Bhawan School.

Through all this uncertainty and change, we continued to think about and discuss new possibilities of suitable education for young children. Dr Mehta too was not satisfied with the conventional pattern Vidya Bhawan had adjusted to—under pressure from the government's grant-in-aid requirements—and was keen to try a new initiative. Eventually, this crystallised into the experiment of Bal Nilaya with Sudesh's leadership, under the aegis of Vidya Bhawan. It was supported by a grant from the National Council for Educational Research and Training (NCERT). This began in 1979. Amita too attended Bal Nilaya for a while before joining the Central School. Bal Nilaya was run as an open learning space in a large room with low tables placed on a carpet. There was no separation of age groups, no bell ringing and no division of school time into periods. Since Amita was the oldest among the 10 or so children, she often helped in guiding the younger ones. This experiment lasted for two years. It received a positive evaluation by NCERT but because of internal differences amongst Vidya Bhawan management, it was not continued. However, Sudesh decided to keep it going on her own as Hans Open School, named thus in memory of her father, Hans Raj Sharma. Parents of the children already in school gave her their full support, pitching in with setting up facilities in new premises in the Polo Ground locality.

A year after we left Seva Mandir, the school shifted to 11A Fatehpura as an adjunct of our residence, and continued there till Sudesh decided to close it in 1989. While it functioned, it did some pioneering and innovative work in open learning, in an atmosphere of mutual support amongst children and between teachers and parents. It also inculcated the values of care for nature through a 'Nature Club'. The school reached a maximum enrolment of 50 with children from different class, religious and linguistic backgrounds. In the late 1980s, some parents became concerned about the lack of formal recognition of the children's achievement through exams and, in their view, the incompatibility of the school's values of cooperation and caring with those prevalent in the business world to which these parents belonged. As a result of this, there were withdrawals and a decline in enrolment, making it unviable to run the school on fees income only. There were also indications of pressure from the state education department for registration and compliance with its rules and regulations. So Sudesh took the decision to close it down.

Tarun's seven years at Mayo College were a mixed experience. He concentrated on his studies, winning awards in English, his favourite subject. My maternal uncle, Col. T. R. Jaitley, was his local guardian during his posting in Ajmer. Tarun spent his weekly day out with this family. We visited Tarun once a month and took him out for treats at popular restaurants. He wrote to us regularly in between these visits. Occasionally, there were incidents of bullying by groups of senior students. Eventually Tarun learnt to stand up to them, which made them desist. This was the unpleasant side of boarding school life for sensitive boys like Tarun. As the Class XII Board Exams approached, Tarun had to face a moral dilemma. One of his classmates claimed to have accessed a leaked exam question paper and was offering to show it to others for a price. Tarun called us on the phone and asked for our guidance. We told him clearly that he should stay clear of such dealings and rely on his own effort to take the exams. He appreciated this and followed our advice. The question paper turned out to be fake. For the Class XII exams, Tarun changed his first choice of subject from Engineering Drawing to English. He was the only student under the guidance of his English teacher, Mr Thakur. He secured 83 per cent marks in English in the Board Exams, which enabled him to get admission to the BA English (Honours) degree course in Hindu College, one of the top colleges at the University of Delhi.

Amita attended Central School till she passed the Class X Board Exams. She cycled 10 kilometres to school twice a day to attend classes and for sports. She also took lessons in Hindustani classical singing. After Class X, she joined Maharani Gayatri Devi (MGD) School in Jaipur, staying in the school hostel. She chose courses in the arts stream for the Class XII exams. In addition, she took active part in cultural activities like dance and theatre. Her local guardians were Bindu Mandawa and family, who were Sudesh's friends from her Uganda days. After appearing for the Class XII exams in 1985, Amita gained admission to the National Institute of Design in Ahmedabad for a five-year course in Graphic and Communication Design.

Prior to the Emergency, my involvement with Gandhian work in the public domain had begun through contacts with Radhakrishna, Secretary of the Gandhi Peace Foundation, Delhi, Dr Ranjit Gupta, an associate of JP, and A. C. Sen, Secretary, Association of Voluntary Agencies for Rural Development (AVARD). I took part in their deliberations and contributed papers on the role of voluntarism in development and social change.

A post-Emergency meeting of voluntary workers with PM Morarji Desai was arranged by Radhakrishna. We were lectured at, not listened to. After the PM's speech, I asked him a question about the possibility of the emergence of a dedicated nonviolent force of cadres in India. He ignored the question and admonished me for my beard.

Other initiatives like Citizens for Democracy, People's Union for Civil Liberties (PUCL), People's Committees, Voters' Councils, Peoples' Candidates and Lokayan were also underway. I became involved in these to varying degrees. A memorable event was the Udaipur Voters' Council initiative for a 'People's Meeting' to hear all candidates for the 1980 parliamentary elections. Many of these efforts did not last due to inner dissensions and ego assertions.

Ever since our return to India in 1972, I had decided to reclaim my Indian citizenship. To do so, I had to renounce my British citizenship since India did not then recognise dual citizenship. I was required to appear in person at the British High Commission in Delhi in 1977. As I handed in my British passport, the British official looked surprised. British citizenship was a prized status and it was rare for anyone to relinquish it. Soon after, I regained my Indian citizenship. A few who came to know this were also surprised, considering it foolish on my part to give up what was, in their eyes, a privilege. This paved the way for a closer involvement with social movements, as we shall see in the chapters to come.

11

Ubeshwar Vikas Mandal

1983–2010

My basic commitment from the 1980s to the early years of the twenty-first century was with the local communities in the Aravalli hills west of Udaipur. There I found a situation of deep crisis, both in terms of the environment and the people. Of course, this had occurred over several decades of political and economic changes that had taken place before and after Independence. My own experience with these communities and my earlier work in Africa and the United States were factors that shaped my relationship and sense of responsibility towards these communities and region. There were other dimensions to this: my own self-recovery and finding a sense of purpose. The self-recovery aspect had to do with my having spent time away from India, from 1949 to 1972. During that time my Indian self, so to say, had become dormant and even arrested in its development. Coming back to India and reconnecting with rural areas took me back to my childhood days of spending holidays in the villages of pre-independence Punjab. I discovered that in certain basic aspects of livelihoods and culture, there were remarkable similarities between what I had grown up with in Punjab in the 1930–40s and what I saw now in Rajasthan. This helped me return to the cultural roots of my Indian self.

The crisis situation and the plight and distress of the people also gave me a sense of purpose for my life at that time. In the 1970s, while doing relief and development work with these communities through the Vidya Bhawan Rural

Institute and Seva Mandir, there was a sense of patronage that these institutions embodied. I felt I had to go beyond that and find a more organic relationship with the communities. Of course, the internal dynamics of these communities, the tensions between the young and the old, the incursions of modern development and governance, the excursions of people into urban life as labourers and semi-skilled workers, as well as the continuities in their traditional way of life, both sacred and secular—all these were factors that shaped my relationship with them.

The reality of Ubeshwar Vikas Mandal (UVM) crystallised as a local group of young men who wanted to open up to new opportunities and take responsibility for this purpose. The founding event of Ubeshwar Vikas Mandal was an all-night *jagran* with bhajan singing on 25–26 January 1983. The 26th of January is celebrated as Republic Day in India, but in my mind, it also held significance for the idea of Gandhian *gram swaraj* or village republics. This idea, I felt, had a basis in the high level of local, self-governing autonomy that existed in these communities, also embodying the more idealistic and reformed idea of *gram swaraj*.

In May 1983, I cut the (umbilical) cord by leaving Seva Mandir and making a start by establishing a direct relation ship with the communities in crisis. Since those tentative, yet concrete beginnings, Ubeshwar Vikas Mandal evolved through many phases as a local community organisation. It was registered under the Societies Registration Act in 1986. Its essential mandate continued to be the ecological and cultural regeneration of the region. For the first two to three years, there were *ad hoc* activities for protection and plantation work in common pastures. Later, larger projects were undertaken for watershed development, soil and water conservation, etc., with the support of the government and international charities.

The first frontline workers were the founding members of UVM—Kesuji Kuria, Gopilal, Radhuji, Nathuji, Navji, Dallaji, Naruji, Kesuji Kher, Gulabji Tawer and Veniram. Kesuji Kuria of Palkhanda can be considered the lead founder of UVM. He had taken the initiative to set up the first mutual help savings group, which established its own rules of functioning. These were reviewed in an annual general meeting and modified when necessary. He had also worked as a literacy instructor with Seva Mandir. Kesuji organised the first group for collective pasture protection in his village. He served as secretary of UVM for many years. Gopilal was a skilled mason who mastered the construction of biogas plants. Radhuji built a *pucca* (permanent) house and made part of it available for UVM's office. Nathuji was an accomplished farmer who brought in new techniques in agriculture. Daljit was the local veterinarian who helped villagers with problems related to domestic animals. Navji introduced the idea and practice of banking through the Vikas Volunteer Vahini scheme of National Bank for Agriculture and Rural Development (NABARD). Kesuji Kher was an accomplished singer and organiser of plays and performances from *Gavri*, the epic dance drama. He also took the lead in acquiring land and building a community-cum-training centre for the area. Gulabji, another expert mason, mobilised the community to contribute labour to build a local temple for the Mother Goddess and an ashram for their local *sadhu*. He also organised fodder distribution in times of drought. Veniram was knowledgeable about traditional farming and the festivals and rituals associated with it.

Later, to deal with the greater technical requirements of the work, professionals were engaged for soil and water conservation, agriculture, animal husbandry, biogas, etc. Administrative and financial management staff had also to be appointed to ensure reporting and accountability for the donors. Throughout this work, certain values were strictly adhered to. Given the widespread corruption in public relief works, we had to make sure that this did not happen in our work. This was ensured through the principle of full payment for a full day's work and openness in record-keeping as well as sharing of such details with the workers.

An effort was also made to introduce literacy and educational activities during the lunch breaks with workers on the sites. Unfortunately, this did not go very far.

Our first major project support came from the National Wasteland Development Board, even though we were not yet formally registered under law as a voluntary organisation. To carry out this work, we were fortunate to get the services of Heera Lal Sharma, who had just left Seva Mandir in 1986. We had worked together in Seva Mandir and I had high regard for his integrity and capacity for field-level organisation. Since our work was expanding into new areas, we needed someone who could make contacts within communities and identify local workers to form organisations and start the work there. He brought our work into the Bagdunda area, about 10 kilometres west of Ubeshwar Temple.

Heera Lal Sharma was with us for only one year. He also brought with him a fellow villager, Ram Chandra Sharma, who took charge of the office and accounts. Ram Chandra continued with us from that time onwards, right up to 2006–07. Even in that short period, Heera Lal Sharma laid the foundation for the essential pattern of community-based work with support from the office in Udaipur. The office was initially in our home at 11A Fatehpura, but later we rented a house across the road from our residence at 10C Fatehpura, where UVM stayed until the early 1990s.

During Heera Lal's time with UVM, we organised a national seminar on the theme 'Aravalli 2001: Prosperity or Disaster'. One of the components of the programme was a meeting of people from villages and from voluntary organisations at Gandhi Ground near Chetak Circle. Heera

Lal-ji was the driving force behind getting nearly 2,000 people to the meeting. The purpose there was to share the conclusions of the seminar with the public at large and to spread the message of the need to protect the forest and pastures in the Aravallis.

After leaving UVM, Heera Lal-ji started his own organisation, named Sahyog. This was located in Kun, east of Udaipur in the plain areas of Mewar. The focus of this work was to support local self-help groups to manage their small savings and gain access to loans from banks to start small home-based enterprises. This continues even today.

Later on, the work of UVM came to be supported by a variety of government and international agencies. To manage this, we had to engage a project in-charge and technical staff for agriculture, soil conservation and afforestation work, and Vishnu Sharma from Ajmer joined us. Vishnu Sharma was also a good organiser, but more at the office level and in relation to contacts with support agencies. He also assisted me in my work with the Ashoka Foundation and took over the responsibility as director after I left this organisation.

Later, Vishnu Sharma joined Inter-Cooperation, a Swiss aid organisation. In that capacity, he continued to provide funding support to UVM. The office-cum-training centre in Bagdunda was built with support from Inter-Cooperation, as were some anicuts in Patiya. This was also watershed development work, including the common pastureland. One of the interesting things that emerged during this work was our discovery of traditional land levelling and field bunding work, undertaken by communities on a mutual-help basis. This was done during the dry season when there were no crops. A group of villagers with contiguous land holdings worked on each small piece of land together. This system is called *arsi-parsi*, the local term for mutual help. This system was also used when constructing new homes, digging common wells, protecting common pastures and even building temples. It is interesting to note that this system was present in many pre-industrial communities all over the world.

In fact, a Russian philosopher/writer, Peter Kropotkin, had written a book titled *Mutual Aid* (1902), which describes this system in Russia during the nineteenth century. I also wrote a small article describing what I saw in Patiya. This was published by *The Indian Express* under the title, 'Aravalli Bhils Show the Way', in the early 1980s. One of the biggest dams built by UVM was constructed on the stream running through Patiya village—as this provided water for irrigation, a canal was also constructed.

The discovery of mutual aid in these communities when doing common work and in pooling their savings for mutual sharing led me to formulate a concept of social organisation. I saw it as a different mode from what I would call institutionalisation. Social organisation is an organic process, which grows out of people living together in small localities and their need to organise for common purposes. Institutionalisation, on the other hand, is a way in which collectivities are formed by top-down bureaucratic, corporate and philanthropic efforts to carry out activities for their development and welfare. I wrote a detailed case study of UVM's work in Patiya and presented it as a paper at a seminar in Chandigarh, held under the aegis of the Department of Sociology, Punjab University. This was later published in a book based on the proceedings of the seminar.

During the 1980s, in addition to full-time workers, we also had volunteers from academic institutions. I especially remember two girls, Roma and Vibha, from the Delhi School of Social Work. They came as part of the volunteer support scheme of the Indian Social Institute, Delhi. Roma and Vibha had a special relationship since Vibha was partially blind, and it was Roma who helped her, both in her daily life routines and with work in the field. We based them in Bagdunda and gave them virtually a free hand to do what they wanted to in the matter of learning and taking initiatives to educate and organise the communities. I think it was a worthwhile exposure and experience for them. I do know that Roma, after a year with us, went on to work with other organisations in north India and became recognised as a major organiser and mobiliser for the causes of people.

Another retired person who joined as a volunteer was the late Mr Bhupinder Bhatia. He was earlier in business, but had been in touch with Anil Sadgopal, a well-known activist-educator who had done pioneering work in science education with young children in rural Madhya Pradesh. Mr Bhatia, through his work with UVM, forged his own connections with people there. He took the initiative to support them with his own resources and improve the assets of individual families, such as farms and wells. This was somewhat different from UVM's approach, which placed greater emphasis on the community rather than on individual families. Eventually Mr Bhatia set himself up as a benefactor in Bagdunda. He even built a small house for himself, where he stayed during his visits to the village.

In the early 1990s, Rajeev Khandelwal from Delhi and Krishna from Bharatpur joined us. They were both close friends. Rajeev Khandelwal took overall charge of UVM as Director while Krishna looked after the work in the field. Krishna tried to knit workers into a coherent team and bring professionalism into the work of UVM. He, like Mr Bhatia, had an entrepreneurial inclination. One of his initiatives was helping a group of local artists and performers of local folk art to become organised and take up activities on their own. This was led by one of UVM's workers, Kesulal Kher, who was himself an accomplished choreographer of folk singing and dancing.

During Rajeev's time at UVM, we also undertook studies of traditional knowledge and practices in the areas of agriculture, land improvement, water conservation, water divining, animal husbandry, etc. Based on these, two small booklets under the title *Living Traditions* were put together with illustrations and text in Hindi and English in the early 1990s. These were team efforts with the primary role given to local knowledgeable people, who could articulate their traditional knowledge and technology in their own language. This was then translated and transcribed into Hindi and English, and illustrations were made based on the observation of actual activities in the field.

During the 1990s, there was considerable interest amongst a group of academics in Chennai, Tamil Nadu, in studying traditional knowledge and technologies. They organised a couple of exhibitions based on this research. UVM took part in one of these gatherings, where our exhibits were put up.

Another study that was conducted was about water sharing in local communities during periods of water scarcity, droughts, etc. This was done by one of our staff, Ram Chandra Sharma, based on knowledge derived from his own village in lower Mewar and supplemented by what he had learnt from local workers Nathuram and Radhu in the Dhar area. This was originally written in Mewari and I made Hindi and English versions.

Rajeev and Krishna also forged their own contacts in the Bagdunda area and even purchased a sizeable piece of land. Eventually they formed their own organisation, called Ajeevika. It focused on seasonal migrant workers who left their villages for urban areas, helping them find jobs, housing and other amenities like education in towns. This initiative later grew into a major organisation that was recognised and supported by the United Nations and other agencies.

In addition to staff and volunteers, we had several collaborations for research related to our work. One of the first was an anthropology teacher from Columbia University in New York, Maxine Weisgrau. Her first study was on the participatory aspect of development in the work of voluntary organisations. For this, she selected Seva Mandir and Ubeshwar Vikas Mandal. I think it was for her PhD work, which was later published as a book. She spent one year here and had to engage an interpreter. Our workers in the field were quite helpful to her.

Her other interest was in the Bhil folk dance-drama known as *Gavri*, and she conducted a number of interviews with local elders and artists who were knowledgeable about this traditional epic. These were carried out initially in Mewari and later translated and transcribed into Hindi and English. She left the notes and transcriptions with UVM. I don't know if she did any further work on it and whether it was published. However, it has been used as a source material for developing a website and a book on *Gavri* by the American activist David Kubiak and colleagues.

I had had a chance to witness *Gavri* performances many years earlier during the 1970s. I was quite fascinated while watching the day-long event, which began with morning prayers and ended with evening prayers. *Gavri* is a folk tradition very peculiar to a particular part of Mewar. Somehow it reminded me of a prototypical form of the classical dance-dramas of Kerala like *Kathakali*, which are based on episodes from the epics.

Gavri is specifically related to the coming of the goddess Parvati in the form of Gauri, the consort of Shiva. It is performed by the men of villages in the region for 40 days after the celebration of Raksha Bandhan.

I often wondered whether there was a way to take *Gavri* to the sophisticated level of a classical dance-drama while maintaining its folk and local roots. Of course, it had evoked interest amongst scholars like Dr Bhanavat and the late Shri Devilal Sharma, founder of Lok Kala Mandal, as well as the artist Baba Goverdanlal Joshi. However, their interest was limited to their own purposes of research, performance in festivals and paintings depicting this form. Beyond these, there did not seem to be any interest in the overall cultural and ecological context of this folk tradition.

Eminent theatre director-playwright Bhanu Bharti took elements of *Gavri* and incorporated them into two of his productions, *Rakta Beej* ('*Blood Seed*') and *Pashu Gayatri*.

During the 1990s, well-known expert in folk traditions, the late Komal Kothari, also became interested in *Gavri*. He was known for his understanding and promotion of the folk singing traditions of Marwar in western Rajasthan, especially amongst the communities of Langas and Manganiyars. These had not only been preserved, but were also revived and refined and had become known internationally. At his initiative, a special performance of an episode of *Gavri* was arranged at the National Centre for Performing Arts (NCPA) in Mumbai at the annual convention of the Bombay Natural History Society.

For this performance, artists from Bagdunda were selected and the renowned theatre director Vijaya Mehta was engaged to choreograph the episode depicting the coming of the Devi, the goddess, accompanied by artistes made up and dressed as wild animals like the tiger, the bear, monkeys, the leopard, and others. Vijaya Mehta spent a whole week working with the local artists, together with Komal Kothari. I accompanied the artistes to Mumbai for the performance and witnessed it. This was the only cultural item for the convention, and it was introduced by the well-known actor Naseeruddin Shah. The purpose of the performance was to drive home the message of the importance of wildlife and its conservation in our folk tradition and the need for conserving this heritage.

After the event, I spoke to Bittu Sehgal, president of the Bombay Natural History Society, to get him interested in the life and culture of the Bhil communities who had kept this tradition alive. I conveyed to him that the future survival of this folk form could only be ensured through the conservation, not only of wildlife, but also of the culture and livelihoods of people who live in the forest in tandem with the wildlife. I have to say with regret that no further interest was shown by this nationally recognised organisation.

Other research partnerships were formed with the Institute of Economic Growth and the Economic Development Associates, Delhi, on participatory development. These were mainly in the form of case studies that actively involved the communities with regard to technical, historical as well as social organisation aspects. Some of these were published in academic journals. One was included in *The Hindu Annual Survey of Environment*. These also provided data for papers presented at seminars and conferences at both the national and international level.

Case studies related to the management of pastures were undertaken in three villages: Keli, Jogion ka Guda and Seedh. These were supported by the Natural Resources Institute (NRI) based in Greenwich, London. Its purpose was to understand the dynamic of the utilisation and sustenance of common forest and pasture lands in these villages. Two of these were selected where UVM had given support to the communities for the protection and regeneration of these lands. The third, Seedh, was selected because of the efforts of the local Sarvodaya worker, who had tried to organise the community as a *gramdaan* village as visualised in the Rajasthan Gramdaan Act of 1971. He, himself a farmer, had been inspired after listening to Vinoba Bhave during his *Padyatra* (a pilgrimage undertaken on foot) in Rajasthan in 1959. He had selected the village Seedh, a little distance from his own village, and explained to this tribal community the idea and legal provisions of gramdaan to become self-managed communities. The Gramdaan Act provides for all land, water, pasture, and forest areas to be brought into the common ownership of the gram sabha. He faced a lot of difficulty in dealing with the local panchayat, revenue and forest officials, but his persistence and sound understanding of the legal provision enabled the community to gain effective control over these resources.

The two villages in the UVM area were selected on the criteria of success and failure. Keli was chosen as the success story, while Jogion ka Guda was chosen as an instance of failure in promoting common land management. The main work of field investigation and study of records and legal aspects was done by Dr Jagdish Purohit, who had by then joined UVM as the director. He had done his PhD in geography and was well-versed in research techniques. He had also worked with my brother, Dr Prem Saint, as a field assistant in the study of wetlands in and around Udaipur during Prem's sabbatical leave in 1994.

For the case studies, a close liaison was maintained between UVM and a representative of scientists from NRI, Greenwich. Unlike some of our earlier experiences with such collaborative work, he was an extremely patient and considerate partner, allowing us full freedom to shape these studies. These were completed within the specified time and published by NRI, giving full credit to all those who contributed their knowledge, right from the village level to UVM staff.

Following the Bhil custom, UVM decided to organise a celebration after the *tirth yatra* and combine it with the commemoration of UVM's registration just over 10 years ago. This was arranged at Ubeshwar Mahadev Temple in the hills above Dhar village. We decided to invite all the villagers in our working area comprising 50 villages, where UVM had contacts. UVM members took responsibility for this and personally went to every village with the invitation. We invited the Tribal Commissioner in Udaipur, Shri Mani from Kerala, as chief guest for the event. Other arrangements included invitations to all the voluntary organisations in Udaipur and the preparation of *prasad* for all the guests. The whole event happened so spontaneously and enthusiastically that I did not have to worry about any of the preparations.

On the day itself, I reached the venue early and oversaw the arrangements for seating, etc. Sudesh accompanied the Commissioner from Udaipur to Ubeshwar in his official car. By around midday, about a few thousand people had gathered—men, women and children dressed in their best clothes. The first part of the function was a procession up to a spring above the temple to perform the ritual of filling the *kalash*. All the women had brought small earthen pots and they gathered at the spring. Ubeshwar members who had gone on the *tirth yatra* and brought back with them *ganga jal* took these to the spring and opened the lids one by one; 101 women from all the villages filled their pots from the spring and a drop of *ganga jal* was added to each pot by the *yatris*. This signified that the pots were now filled with the holy water of the Ganga.

As soon as this was completed, a procession, accompanied by the beating of drums and cymbals, began to return to the temple. Now the women were carrying the *kalash*es on their heads and some of them began to sway as if they were moved by the spirit of the goddess Ganga and had to be supported by others with them. Sudesh and I also joined the procession, with Sudesh carrying a *kalash* on her head. At the temple, everyone was seated for the next part of the celebration.

The commissioner and other guests addressed the gathering and conveyed their appreciation for and encouragement of the work that the people had been doing in their villages for the protection and regeneration of the forest. Among the other guests were Mohan Singh Kothari, one of the trustees of Seva Mandir, and a *sadhu* known by the name of Maunibaba (as he had taken a vow of silence for 12 years). He was from Haryana, and was staying at the temple.

A report on the 10 years of UVM work was read out by Ram Chandra Sharma and I addressed the gathering to thank everyone for their cooperation. After the function, everyone was given a platter of *prasad*, which consisted of *googri*, a sweet preparation made from boiled wheat grains and jaggery lightly fried in *ghee*. We had no idea how many people would turn up, but miraculously, no one left without the *prasad*. A reporter from the *Rajasthan Patrika* was also there—he took photographs and the next day a report was published in the local edition of the paper.

The last event that UVM organised was a seminar on drought and desertification under the aegis of Sir Dorabji Tata Trust. Its director, Mukund Gorakshkar, personally came to attend it. Its objective was to bring the voluntary organisations in Udaipur together to develop a common understanding about the vulnerability to drought in the region and plan a concerted action to deal with the situation. The seminar was arranged at a hotel near Chetak Circle, which provided facilities such as conference rooms. We had made careful preparations around the theme, with a presentation outlining the causes, conditions and possible solutions of the problem of drought. All the major voluntary organisations had been invited, together with a few university academics who had studied the problem and tried to develop appropriate technologies. My initial presentation was illustrated by a wall display of the main sub-themes of the seminar—causes, conditions and solutions. After this, the participants shared their experiences, followed by the views of soil and water conservation experts from the college of technology and agricultural engineering and the department of geography of ML Sukhadia University. Mukund appreciated the inputs from the participants and recommended that a coordinating body be set up to promote collective action by the voluntary sector, with the promise that if this came about, his trust would be glad to consider supporting such an initiative. Regretfully, I have to say that this did not come about. I am yet to understand why.

12

Ashoka Foundation, India

1984–89

In the 1980s, while I kept in touch with Ubeshwar Vikas Mandal, occasionally visiting Dhar on cycle or by bus, an unexpected avenue opened up. Late in 1984 I received a phone call from Kirtee Shah, a friend of our colleague Kamla Bhasin. He was an architect practising in Ahmedabad who was also involved in social work. He knew I had left Seva Mandir. He asked me if I would be interested in working as Director of Ashoka Foundation (AF) in India and if I could come for an interview with Ashok Advani, the president of AF's India chapter. I was taken aback, but appreciated the suggestion. I knew little about the organisation or the job. I travelled to Bombay to find out more. I met Ashok Advani at his office in central Bombay. He owned and edited *Business India*, an influential weekly magazine. Ashok was warm and friendly. He explained the job responsibilities and had no questions of his own. Apparently, he had been told about my background by Kirtee Shah and they had decided to offer me the job. He stressed that he saw my joining as the forging of a lasting relationship with the organisation. When he asked me how much remuneration I expected, I replied that Rs 2,000 would be adequate. He was surprised, but also glad that I was adhering to my value of frugality. I clarified to him that I had concerns and commitments in the Udaipur region that I would continue to be engaged with. My base would remain in Udaipur even as I took up my new role as director-cum-fellow in the Ashoka Fellowship Programme.

Ashoka Foundation was founded in the USA by William Drayton, a Harvard Business School (HBS) and Peace Corps alumnus with independent means. He wished to support international entrepreneurs in public service, who were termed 'Innovators for Public'. A chapter had been started in India with the help of Ashok Advani, also an HBS alumnus and friend of Bill Drayton. After functioning for a few years, it had run into trouble, with policy differences emerging amongst the Board and the resignation of the director. When I took over, I had to start from scratch and rebuild the organisation. This involved reviving the database of contacts and redesigning the selection process and support framework for the fellowship programme. Here, my experience with FWC as director of its independent study programme came in handy. However, the biggest help came from Bill Drayton, who had over several years honed a methodology for the selection of fellows. He always made the effort to be present for all interviews and Board meetings, where he compulsively ate—literally—baskets full of oranges! AF had his exclusive commitment all these years. As a fellowship, it is now functioning in over 95 countries.

For the first round of selections, I visited Maharashtra, Kerala, Bangalore and Andhra Pradesh. I saw the work of Vivek and Vidyutlata Pandit to free bonded labourers, as well as Shanti and Satish Nair engaged in highlighting biodiversity and conservation problems in the Western Ghats. Lastly, I saw the efforts of my friend Dr Parameshwara Rao in enabling natural regeneration in degraded hill areas of the Eastern Ghats near Visakhapatnam. I shared with him the plight of the Aravallis due to deforestation, and sought his advice. He took me to a hill called Panchdarla and showed me the natural regeneration that had taken place in five years just by protecting the area from free grazing. There was now enough fodder to run a dairy and obtain fuelwood to meet the needs of the local community. He felt that if this could happen there, it could also be replicated in the Aravallis. For me, this proved to be the demonstration and encouragement I desperately needed at that time of near despair about the situation in Mewar region.

Back in Udaipur, I shared my observation of Panchdarla Hill with Kesuji Kuria of Palkhanda. I suggested to him that if a sizeable plot of degraded pasture could be identified in Dhar, we could attempt a similar demonstration of natural regeneration in their area. Over the next few months, Kesuji discussed the possibility in his hamlet. He was able to convince 16 farmers with individual contiguous smallholdings of pastureland to pool these together as a single pasture, around which would be built a protection wall. They were prepared to do the work, but did not have the required resources. Regardless, some of them began to construct a dry stone wall around the perimeter. In the following summer vacations, a group of Tarun's friends from Hindu College came to stay in Dhar for village study. One of them, Manik Mahna, was moved by the people's voluntary effort. On his return to Delhi, he raised funds from family and friends to support this work. This was the first public donation received by UVM. The protection wall was completed before the rains. That season brought average rainfall—enough to make the grasses and shrubs sprout. Since grazing had been eliminated, the grasses flourished, providing enough fodder for small farmers' livestock for the whole year. Before harvesting the fodder, farmers from Dhar Patti were invited to see this demonstration. They were impressed and keen to undertake similar work in their villages. However, the problem of lack of funds remained. Fortunately, this was solved through some important changes in thinking and policy about land degradation at the national level.

In the early 1980s, the results of a survey conducted by an independent body, Society for Promotion of Wasteland Development (SPWD), were made public. These revealed that about two-thirds of land resources in India had become degraded, with diminishing productivity. The central government, under Prime Minister Rajiv Gandhi's leadership, recognised the seriousness of the problem and set up the National Wasteland Development Board, an autonomous body under the Ministry of Environment and Forests. It was mandated to promote and support government and non-government efforts in the restoration and improvement of degraded lands.

I approached the Chairperson, Dr Kamla Chowdhry, whom I had met at a seminar, and briefed her on the situation in the Aravallis of southern Rajasthan. I invited her to visit our area and see it for herself. To her credit, she readily agreed and arranged a visit. I accompanied her in the field and showed her the barren hills with vanishing soil and the onset of gully erosion. I also showed her the initiative for pastureland protection by the community in Palkhanda hamlet. She was impressed. On the spot she sanctioned a grant of nearly Rs 900,000 for UVM to extend the land improvement work to other villages. UVM was not yet registered under the Societies Registration Act at the time, and thus not eligible for government funds. Kamla Chowdhry overruled this and sanctioned the grant for UVM as a special case. This enabled UVM to engage full-time staff for technical and administrative purposes and to support the communities' labour. It also propelled me into the environment movement at the national level. More on that will be discussed in due course.

Meanwhile, AF's work gained momentum. Programme fellows were selected twice a year. I made it a point to visit promising candidates and see their work in the field. After that, those shortlisted were invited for rigorous interviews over three days. Bill Drayton, Ashok Advani and Kirtee Shah were always present. Usually, experts with a wide range of experience were also invited. Once a year, a retreat was arranged for selected fellows to share their experiences and offer suggestions for improving AF's policy and process. In the mid-1980s, I began a newsletter titled *Changemakers* to share news of the progress amongst fellows and the wider community. In the opening issue, I wrote the editorial, defining the concept of 'Social Entrepreneurship'. This was also published as an article in IIM Ahmedabad's magazine *Vikalpa*, titled 'Enterprise and Innovation in Constructive Work'.

Through this, the term 'social enterprise' gained wide currency and was adopted by other fellowship programmes. I continued with AF for five years. During that time, I tried to persuade the Board to make AF more grounded in and relevant to the Indian context. This did not succeed due to Bill Drayton's unwillingness to decentralise and the failure of other members to create India-sourced means of funding the programme. As a result, I left the organisation in 1989.

13

The 1980s and Onward

Along with my work with UVM, I also took an interest in and lent support to several movements and issues related to communities and the environment. One of these was the well-known Narmada Bachao Andolan (NBA), which emerged during the mid-1980s under the leadership of Medha Patkar. Medha had visited us when she was a student at Tata Institute of Social Sciences (TISS), Mumbai. At that time we had discussed her concerns and ways to get involved in social action. I don't know exactly how her involvement with NBA came about; my guess is that it was essentially due to the plight that awaited the communities living in different parts of the Narmada Valley as a result of the scores of dams being constructed on the Narmada and its tributaries. The largest of the dams was to be constructed near Kevadia and was to be named Sardar Sarovar Dam.

The whole scheme was modelled on the great river valley projects like the Tennessee Valley Authority, which had been carried out in the United States during the inter-war years. These were supposed to be multipurpose projects for irrigation, hydroelectric power generation and watershed development. An earlier example of this in India is the Damodar Valley Project in eastern India. The problem in the case of the River Narmada was that it was an extensively settled area, with agricultural communities along the flood plains and forest dwellers on the ridges and hills surrounding them. Construction of the dams inevitably led to the submergence of the lower parts of the valleys and, in some cases, the middle forested regions as well.

This meant that the inhabitants of these areas had to be displaced and relocated. Their numbers ran into thousands of villages and hundreds of thousands of people. The projects did have provisions for the resettlement of these people, but proper implementation was often missing. As I said, these were the concerns which I think motivated Medha Patkar to throw herself wholeheartedly into the cause of these communities.

Along with others from outside the area, I became interested in the Andolan partly for reasons of solidarity with Medha, but mainly due to the magnitude of the problem being created and the precedent being set for destructive trends in development, both for people and the environment. Our interest took the form of periodic visits to the valley to join the ongoing rallies and protest.

Let me mention some of the highlights of my engagement. During one of the visits, I accompanied Dr Brahmadev Sharma, an IAS officer, who was at that time Commissioner for Scheduled Castes and Scheduled Tribes in the central government. This is an autonomous agency mandated to monitor the policies and programmes related to Scheduled Castes and Scheduled Tribes and make reports on them to the government.

Dr Sharma was indeed unique amongst the officers in that he wore a traditional kurta and dhoti and made it a point to visit the areas where these communities faced problems due to development. During our visit, we had to cross the Narmada. This was the dry season so the flow was at a low level. We crossed it in a boat, which the boatmen guided by pulling the vessel along a rope-cable strung across both sides of the river's banks. We crossed from the northern bank to the southern bank of the river because Medha and her workers were staying there in a tribal village.

Even though it was the dry season, we had to trek a few kilometres through wetlands along the river. We arrived as dusk was falling and spent the night there. The next day, Dr Sharma decided to take on the role of an activist and asked all the workers to take a pledge to save the river by refusing to shift even when the water rose after the dam construction. One of their slogans was '*Koi nahi hatega, Bandh nahi banega!*' ('No one will give ground, no dam will be built!').

Even as the protests and rallies continued, the construction work, too, continued apace. A year or two later, as the waters began to rise behind the dam, Medha shifted to a site where there was a temple called Shulpaneshwar. That year the rains were quite heavy and the site that Medha was occupying was expected to be submerged. Medha decided that regardless of what happened, she would not move from that place.

When I learnt about this, I decided that I had to go and be with her on the occasion. Accompanied by another activist, Ramesh Billorey, we reached the site. There were constant warnings of the imminent rising waters and we could see the water visibly nearing the hut where Medha was staying. The whole night was spent in anticipation of what might happen, although there was no anxiety. The seven or eight of us present felt a sense of peace throughout the night; rather, we had a sense of satisfaction and peace at the opportunity to sacrifice ourselves for this larger cause.

There was no attempt to rescue us, no boats, and no policemen. We were with each other and in the hands of fate. I slept very peacefully that night. I've had no recurrence of an experience of that kind.

The next morning, when we woke up, providentially the water had not risen beyond the threshold of the final steps leading to our site.

Another memorable occasion was when a group of us travelled from Udaipur to Kevadia to support Medha during one of her fasts for the cause of the Narmada. This was at the Kevadia Colony. As we neared the place of her fast, we were stopped by the Gujarat Police and asked where we were going. We decided to be truthful and told them that we were going to Kevadia. They immediately took us into custody and drove to the police station at Rajpipla. There were scores of others also being detained. Each of us had to give our name and address. After that, we were taken to the jail located inside an old fort.

We spent two days and two nights there. We were left alone and spent our time singing and sharing experiences and concerns. Overall, we were treated quite cordially by the jailer. On the third day, Medha arrived and we were allowed to leave the jail.

Even though the NBA had a few successes—like ensuring proper resettlement and rehabilitation of the displaced communities, as well as being able to stop the World Bank funding of the main project, the Sardar Sarovar Dam—overall it could not claim to be a success. The struggle still goes on, with demands to limit raising the height of the dam. Medha eventually became involved in larger issues and the broader concerns of development and the environment, and provided leadership in the National Alliance for People's Movements. Our most recent meeting with her was when she came to visit us in 2018. Despite her lifelong commitment to these causes and the hard work and strain involved, she seemed to be in good health. She is more engaged in writing and sharing her experiences now.

In the early 1980s, I had become involved in Lokayan, a dialogue between intellectuals and activists initiated by the late political scientist Rajni Kothari. This was based in the Centre for Study of Developing Societies (CSDS) and was supported by a German foundation. It included independent-minded intellectuals like social psychologist Ashis Nandy, sociologist Dhirubhai Sheth, political scientist Giri Deshingkar, China expert Mira Sinha, political philosopher Ramashray Roy and scholar-activists like Jayant Bandopadhyay, Vandana Shiva, Rajni Bakshi, Narendranath, Smitu Kothari, Vijay Pratap,

Avdhesh Kumar, Claude Alvares and others. I was an active participant and contributed several papers for seminars and the *Lokayan Bulletin*. These included writings on themes like Gandhi's 'Hind Swaraj', the plight of Adivasis, agents and agencies of change. For me, it was a wonderful opportunity to interact with India's top public intellectuals on issues and concerns I was engaged in.

There was also a point of disagreement with Rajni Kothari. He wrote an article in *Lokayan Bulletin* reviewing the role of voluntary agencies, in which he criticised me and others for accepting government support for community work and thus being co-opted. I wrote back, defending our position and sense of responsibility in providing support to communities in times of distress. My response was taken in the right spirit and published in full in the *Lokayan Bulletin*. During review meetings, there were heated exchanges on the question of Lokayan participants' relationship with political parties and their use of that forum for party work. Overall, opinion remained against such use. Lokayan maintained its role as a non-party political process focused on dialogue, documentation and communication. After Lokayan, I continued to engage in dialogue with intellectuals/activists— Ashis Nandy, J. P. S. Uberoi, K. R. Datye, Alok Bhalla, Sudhir Chandra, Ramchandra Guha, Aseem Srivastava and Ashish Kothari.

During the 1980s and 1990s, there were several protests and demonstrations on environmental issues and the plight of the people affected by pollution and the degradation of natural resources. One very prolonged protest was the resistance to the construction of the Mansi-Wakal Dam in the Jhadol area. This was a project undertaken with the support of Hindustan Zinc Limited, the major public-sector industrial enterprise in Udaipur District. A large dam was to be constructed in a valley through which two tributaries of the Sabarmati, the Mansi and the Wakal, flowed. The resistance came from the villages whose lands were likely to be submerged by the waters of the dam. This protest was led by Ganesh Purohit, who came from one of the villages. It lasted for nearly nine years. At one point, there was also a violent altercation between the villagers and the police during a *dharna* at the dam site.

Initially, almost all the water was intended for Hindustan Zinc Limited, but later it was decided that one-third of the water would be provided for domestic purposes to Udaipur city. The scheme involved lifting water from one watershed to another, bringing it to Pichhola Lake in Udaipur by pipeline. Eventually the matter was settled through an agreement to provide compensatory land and adequate compensation to the affected people in the area.

Another protest movement was against ground and surface water pollution by a chemical factory producing H-acid, a carcinogenic chemical used in textile dyeing. Apparently, the factory, situated not far from a Hindustan Zinc Limited smelter at Debari, had not taken any measures to treat or dispose of its waste products. All the waste was being piled up near the factory, inside its compound. As a result, during the first rains in 1989, the chemical waste, which is highly soluble, began to flow out of the premises into the lands and canals downstream. The worst affected were the farmers of Bichhdi village as the water in their wells and canals began to take on a brownish-purple colour. People called it 'Coca-Cola' coming out of the ground. Even the concrete-lined canals were eroded by this highly acidic effluent.

The situation was brought to the notice of Manna Ram Dangi, a lawyer who had been my student at Vidya Bhawan Rural Institute. He told me about what was happening and invited me to visit the area. I went there and was appalled to see the damage that had been done within a few months of the functioning of the factory. People had begun protesting, but the owner and upstart entrepreneur paid no attention to them.

I then decided to contact my friend Anil Agarwal, the editor of *Down to Earth*, who was an alumnus of the Indian Institute of Technology, Kanpur, and apprised him of the situation. He, in turn, contacted his teacher, Dr G. D. Agarwal. Both of them came to Bichhdi and were also shocked to see what had happened.

Following this, a decision was made to visit the engineering college at Roorkee where Dr Agarwal was acquainted with people specialising in the study of groundwater pollution. They invited me to accompany them and together we made a presentation there. The college decided to send a team of scientists to assess the damage that had been done and a report was prepared. Meanwhile, Manna Ram Dangi also lodged a complaint with the local administration. The Assistant District Magistrate concerned did pass an order, but there was insufficient evidence to take effective action against the factory.

On the basis of the Roorkee scientists' report, the matter was taken up to the Supreme Court by a Delhi-based Supreme Court lawyer, M. C. Mehta. I had a chance to visit the United States during that time. My trip included a meeting with Sidney Harman, the industrialist who had served as the president of Friends World College and with whom I had worked closely. He had been the under-secretary of commerce under the President of the United States, Jimmy Carter, in the late 1970s. With his help, I was able to meet the officials in the Environment Protection Agency in Washington, DC and get from them exact information about H-acid and its process of manufacture, as well as the hazards if its untreated effluents are released. I shared these with the Supreme Court via Shri M. C. Mehta as well as with Anil Agarwal.

At the local level, I took part in meetings of the villagers in Bichhdi organised by Manna Ram to apprise them of what was being done to deal with the problem as well as further action they could take. From time to time, there were demonstrations in front of the factory, Hindustan Agrochemicals Limited. I took part in some of them. On one occasion, the owner, at our insistence, asked us to come inside the factory compound to show us that no effluents were being released. He pinned the whole blame for the pollution on the nearby Hindustan Zinc Limited smelter. He even claimed that the liquid effluent was harmless; he asked for a glassful to be brought to him and announced that he was prepared to drink it. At the same time, he added that if anything happened, we would be responsible. We looked around the compound and could see growing heaps of solid waste at the back of the factory. This was where the pollution came from whenever it rained, because H-acid and its by-products, as mentioned earlier, are highly soluble.

The court cases dragged on over decades; despite orders from the higher level to remove the solid waste, restore the damaged land and water resources, and pay compensation to the villagers, nothing substantial happened. Recently, in 2019, I heard from Manna Ram that the owner had lodged a court case against the villagers, accusing them of defaming him and causing him losses in his enterprise.

Another movement I was involved in was initiated by Dr Brahmdev Sharma, who had retired as a central govern-ment civil servant. During his service, he had become something of a legend for upholding the cause of tribal and Scheduled Caste welfare. He had had postings as Collector in Bastar district in Madhya Pradesh, where he tried to ensure that tribal interests were protected and that the benefits of schemes intended for them reached them. Later, he became a Commissioner for Scheduled Castes and Scheduled Tribes in the central government. In this capacity, he wrote detailed reports about how tribal interests had been betrayed and legal provisions meant to protect them had not been adhered to. Before retirement, he was appointed the

Vice Chancellor of North-Eastern Hill University, Shillong. There, he wrote many books and pamphlets highlighting the problems of tribals.

After retirement, during the 1990s, Dr Sharma acted as an advisor to the Bhuria Committee, which had been mandated to look into the situation of tribal communities and propose measures for undoing historical and present-day injustices. As a result of their recommendations, a new Panchayati Raj Extension to Scheduled Areas (PESA) Act was passed in the mid-1990s. Dr Sharma was the key figure involved in drafting it. He brought into this the Gandhian concept of *gram swaraj*, 'village republics', for tribal areas by making the village assembly or *gram sabha* the key body (instead of the panchayat), the ultimate authority in deciding the affairs and development in the villages. The Act also provided that a village would be recognised as defined by the community itself instead of the revenue department, as was the case in general. There is also a provision for community rights and community resources, apart from the individual family holdings.

In order to promote the people's involvement, Dr Sharma launched a movement called Bharat Jan Andolan. For this, he produced many pamphlets in simple Hindi and English to educate the workers and communities about their rights. The Udaipur region was one of the areas he selected for pilot efforts for the people-led *gram swaraj* movement. Here, he was in touch with three organisations—Astha, Jagran Jan Vikas Samiti and Ubeshwar Vikas Mandal. He made regular visits to our areas of work in Udaipur and Dungarpur Districts, meeting workers and addressing public assemblies.

As I have mentioned, unlike other civil servants who are suited and booted, he was always dressed in a traditional white dhoti and kurta. I had the chance to have long conversations with him and learnt a great deal from his experience and knowledge.

His last assignment was to bring about a dialogue between the government and extreme left-wing Naxalite groups in the forest of Bastar. As a result of his meetings with the Naxalites, an understanding was reached about the terms on which they would end their anti-government operations. However, soon after his return from a visit to the area, he heard that the understanding had been violated and there had been violence on both sides. He was deeply disappointed—this even affected his mental health and in his last years, he became quite incoherent in conversation.

At the field level in UVM, we took up the work of spreading the message of PESA in our area. In a few selected villages, the communities, guided by our members and workers, took the decision to declare themselves as 'Gram Swaraj Villages' and put up concrete slabs with the provisions of the *gram sabha*'s powers and rights written on them. This was essentially an expression of their intention to become self-existent and self-defined communities with inalienable rights and responsibilities for the care and management of their private and common land, water, forest and wildlife, and livestock within the village boundaries. These boundaries were marked by pillars at key points along the perimeter of the village.

The understanding and sentiment about this 'self-being', *swayambhu,* and commonality varied across village communities. The strongest in this respect was in a remote village of 50–60 households named Keli, located at the headwaters of a stream that flowed westwards into Ruparel, a tributary of the Sabarmati. The declaration of 'Gram Swaraj' in this village was made in the presence of one of the top leaders of the Sarvodaya Movement, Sidhhraj Dhadha, and a local Gandhian, Deendayal Dashottar. Within the village, cohesion and strength were provided by a traditional leader, Hakraji Gameti, and his son Prem. They were able to convince the forest department that they were capable of taking care of their pastures and forest lands and needed to be trusted. The department official, Shri Soni, understood this and cooperated with the villagers, consulting them regularly for the management of forest areas and sharing the produce with them. UVM also took up the work of watershed development, involving bunding, land-levelling, checking dam construction, and building an anicut with a lift-irrigation facility for lands upstream. Later, we did a case study of the whole effort for the Natural Resource Institute based in Greenwich, London.

Along with the work on gram *ganraj* through PESA, UVM continued its other activities, like community-based watershed development with support from international agencies like Caritas Switzerland, the Norwegian Agency for Development Cooperation (NORAD), Oxfam Great Britain (GB) and Sir Dorabji Tata Trust.

At one point, UVM became involved in the issue of damage resulting from mining in the Aravallis. Mining had expanded rapidly during the 1980s and 1990s because of the demand for building stones in India as well as for export. In areas adjacent to the main roads, all the way from Rajsmand to Kherwada, mainly marble of different hues and quality was being mined. This was mostly open-cast mining, initially done manually by labourers, most of whom were tribals, who lived on the sites. We visited some of these workers and saw their miserable living conditions, sleeping in makeshift huts made from stone slabs that were barely 4 feet high, usually built into the recesses of hillsides that had been hollowed out by mining. Later on, machines were introduced and the scale of mining increased. I've seen whole hillsides stripped away and some of the old settlements, in one case even part of an old palace, mined away.

UVM organised a meeting of different agencies to highlight the problem and brought out a small report. As in the case of other problems related to environmental damage, legislative action has been undertaken by the government, but enforcement has been very weak.

Some of my other involvements included the 'Jungle, Jameen, Jan Andolan' to press for the rights of tribal people on forest lands, the Jheel Sanrakshan Samiti concerned with pollution of the lakes, rivers and streams of Udaipur due to the discharge of untreated sewages, as well as meetings to promote cooperation and collective action among voluntary agencies in Udaipur.

In the late 1990s, I was contacted by David Selvaraj of Visthar in Bangalore. His organisation had been conducting three-month, semester-long courses from Concordia and Gustavus Aldolfus Colleges in Wisconsin. Their courses were shaped around the themes of development, environment and justice, and included both lectures and field studies. David was looking to diversify the course by including some time in an area in north India. He asked me if UVM could take this on and host the group for a 10-day programme. This attracted me and sort of led me back to my work in Friends World College, which David knew about, so we took this opportunity and for 10 years, I organised the Rajasthan component of their course single-handedly. We made arrangements for them to stay at a modest accommodation called Hotel Meera, which had conference room facilities. I explained the whole purpose and design of the programme to the proprietor, and I'm happy to say that he was fully cooperative and provided the best of Rajasthani hospitality in a highly courteous and caring manner. For the course, I invited lecturers from universities and colleges in Udaipur. I also set up a library in the conference room using my own books and some which I borrowed from Shikshantar. For fieldwork, we took the students to villages and worksites in the UVM area. At the end of each course, we asked the students to evaluate various components and their overall experience of the course. This feedback was generally encouraging and indicated that the time they had spent with us had contributed to deepening their understanding of issues related to the themes of development, environment and justice.

This quasi-academic work on my part became known to other organisations in Udaipur which had been hosting groups for short-term courses for various colleges from the US. There were organisations like Foundation for Sustainable Development (FSD), Foundation for Ecological Sustainability (FES), Seva Mandir and, more recently, Jagran. They invited me to hold talks for the students during the orientation period, before they took up project work with a local NGO. I prepared notes and PowerPoint presentations for these talks on the themes of the genealogy of development with its roots in colonialism, and the idea of colonialism and related concepts of the civilising mission, the white man's burden and progress. I also brought in the issue of sustainability in present-day development and how to give it a sound participatory and indigenous basis, building on the ideas and work of Mahatma Gandhi.

My last international engagement was with the World Bank (WB) for a consultation with activists from around the world on their rural development policies. This was at the initiative of Mr Reddy, who had recently been appointed as the WB liaison for its outreach to civil society. It was a three-day event in 2003, arranged in a country mansion converted into a conference centre in the idyllic English countryside of Oxfordshire. It began with a presentation of WB perspectives and policies on rural development, followed by responses from the activists. In general, the opinion was that the intended benefits were not reaching the poorest people. The recipient countries' approach tended to be top-down rather than participatory. Some were even critical of the WB giving support to regimes that were authoritarian, and which regularly violated human rights. I circulated my presentation based on a paper I had prepared earlier under the title, 'Rethinking Participation'. All the opinions expressed were taken note of and assurance was given that these would be considered while framing future policies for rural development.

No one expected any concrete outcome. For me, it was a good opportunity to meet activists from other continents and WB officials. The hospitality was warm and I enjoyed my walks and talks in the spacious grounds of the estate.

The 1980s was a decade when concern for the environment emerged on a widespread scale in India. This was initially led by professionals like Anil Agarwal, Sunita Narayan, and Ravi Chopra, who made a careful study of the state of India's environment and brought out, with wide-ranging collaboration from the field, several editions of reports on the state of India's environment. A Hindi edition of the first report was put together by Anupam Mishra of the Gandhi Peace Foundation.

Issues related to the environment became the preoccupation of the central and state governments—ministries were set up and legislation passed to deal with them. I was able to take part in the deliberations of various committees, both with autonomous organisations and with government institutions. This work entailed a lot of travel to different parts of the country as well as internationally. These are too numerous to recount; however, the one that stands out is my visit to Lahore in Pakistan for an environment-related conference. It was integral to the thinking of voluntary environment movements that this issue be seen on a subcontinental basis and beyond. To this thinking I contributed an article, titled 'The Ecological Imperative in South Asia', which was published in *The Indian Express*. During the visit to Lahore, we could not travel to any other place. At the conclusion of the conference, we were asked to give some feedback. I took the opportunity to convey to the participants and to the hosts that I was born and had been brought up in my early years in and around Peshawar and Rawalpindi. I said that with those roots, I could not bring myself to consider Pakistan an enemy. This seemed to stun the hosts, who were accustomed to the adversarial positions that had developed between the two countries, but at the same time, it was appreciated.

During the early 1980s I worked closely with Anil Agarwal and we discussed the possibility of forming a Green Party in India. He, however, had a different agenda and, as a journalist, was keen on launching a magazine which could study and raise environment issues on sound technical and scientific grounds. This took the form of the fortnightly *Down to Earth*, published by the Centre for Science and Environment. This effort continues up to the present day and is recognised as a reliable and authoritative contribution to environmental investigative journalism and advocacy.

With Agarwal and others, I also attended conferences and a seminar in Paris in the late 1980s. These were preparatory discussions for addressing the interface between the environment and development issues. A commission had been set up to study this aspect under the chairperson, the Norwegian Prime Minister Gro Brundland, with Dr Manmohan Singh (who was later Prime Minister of India) as the secretary. The commission published a report called 'Our Common Future', in which it declared that the present course of development was not sustainable and ways must be found to move to a sustainable path of economic development. This report played an important part in the Rio de Janeiro conference on environment and development in 1991, where sustainability was included as the key theme in its report, 'Agenda 21'.

Apart from this, I also had the occasion to visit Germany at the invitation of a sociologist friend, Sarma Marla, a professor at the University of Frankfurt. Anupam Mishra was the other invitee during this visit. We spent a whole week with Sarma

Marla and his wife, Irmal, in a village community in south Germany, discussing and recording different aspects of the social, political and cultural ramifications of environmental issues. During our breaks, we took a round of the village and saw the water supply and wastewater treatment system, starting with the purification plant for water from the River Rhine, its supply to households through different pipelines for drinking, domestic and cleaning purposes, to the treatment plants and release into plantations.

Other visits included our trips to Finland during 1990–91 at the invitation of philosophy professor Thomas Wallgran and his students at the University of Helsinki. This was in the summer and we had the experience of seeing the sun remain above the horizon for 20 hours a day. We also saw the waste management arrangements for sorting out solid household waste, visited organic farms and met a person trying to preserve the traditional ship-building technology and musical instruments like the *kantele*. Thomas and some of the students visited us in Udaipur and saw the work of Ubeshwar Vikas Mandal.

Together with a concern about the degradation of nature through development-related deforestation, droughts and water scarcity, and soil erosion, there was also anxiety about the impact of all these changes on local rural, especially tribal, communities. Broadly speaking, two major streams of thinking and effort emerged in relation to the environment— one focusing on conservation and protection of nature and the other focusing on the plight of the communities dependent on nature for their livelihood. These streams were apparent both in official and non-official circles.

One of the better-known organisations in the conservation community at that time was Kalpavriksh, founded by Ashish Kothari, the youngest son of political scientist Rajni Kothari. Ashish's initial emphasis was on nature conservation, but as a result of our conversation during a seminar, where I stressed the integral relationship between local rural and tribal communities and nature, he grasped the point about the importance of communities. He has acknowledged that since then, he has thought, campaigned and written about community-based nature conservation. Over the past two years, we have revived our relationship.

At the international level, I was invited to become a member of the Advisory Committee for Oxfam, Great Britain, in India. In this capacity, I was invited to visit England and Scotland in order to promote a publication titled *Development in Practice*, which highlighted the ground-level work being supported by Oxfam in different parts of the world. During my visit, meetings were arranged with Oxfam staff and supporters in different cities—Oxford, London, Bristol, Edinburgh, etc. At these meetings, I tried to present what I called the 'worm's eye-view', as distinct from the 'bird's eye view.' This phrase initially raised eyebrows, but after my presentation, there was some change in understanding the viewpoint of the people and workers at the grassroots level.

During the 1990s, Oxfam had launched two initiatives to bring about some major changes in its working. On the one hand, in India, there was a move towards an Indianisation of Oxfam. Globally, on the other hand, there was a move for internationalising its concerns. A proto-Oxfam India was floated and Oxfam International was set up with headquarters in Oxford.

As part of the parallel process of Indianisation of Oxfam, the aim was to help the emergence of Oxfam India, with initial support from Oxfam GB. I was invited to be a member of the board for this. Other members were Oxfam GB staff working in India and a few Oxfam partners. Soon differences cropped up in the board meetings between those who wanted complete autonomy for Oxfam India and others who wanted to maintain Oxfam GB's oversight. I supported the former group. While these discussions continued, an executive director was appointed and fundraising activities initiated in India. At one point, it became obvious that the differences could not be reconciled, so those who favoured the continued oversight of Oxfam GB decided to leave the board.

Fundraising in India became a problem and a new executive director named Ramappa was brought in. He had been one of the regional directors of Oxfam GB in India and was a very committed and dynamic person. He had contact with the Swedish International Development Agency (SIDA) and brought in a huge project with focus on water management. For some time, this work and other initiatives, like support for relief work in Gujarat after the earthquake in 2001 and work to promote communal harmony in Hyderabad and other areas, made considerable headway. However, serious problems emerged between the chairman of the board, Murray Culshaw, and Ramappa. These were mainly around fundraising—Murray was not happy with the overwhelming dependence on foreign funds and was in favour of greater effort in fundraising and communication in India. Since these differences could not be resolved, Murray decided to resign and I was asked to take over the chair of Oxfam India.

Meanwhile, Oxfam GB, with the support of the group that had resigned from Oxfam India, set up another Oxfam India. As a result, an issue arose about our continuing to use the name, because Oxfam was a recognised trademark both in the UK and internationally. Some of the members of our board were in favour of making it a legal issue, but I was in any case not happy with continuing with the name Oxfam, so I persuaded the Board to surrender the name and get ourselves registered with a different name. This was finalised as 'SVARAJ', an acronym standing for Society for Voluntary Action, Revitalization and Justice.

The work for water management funded by SIDA continued for a while, but progress was rather slow because of Ramappa's tendency to take on other urgent issues. In one of the review meetings for the SIDA project with their representative in India, it became clear that SIDA was not satisfied and was considering withholding the funding. This precipitated a crisis, with the Board deciding to provide additional support to Ramappa for SIDA's project. Again, there were problems regarding relations between the new advisor, Pradeep, an experienced person especially in relief work, and Ramappa. Eventually, Ramappa was asked to step down. Pradeep continued in the leadership role for a while, but made it clear that this was only temporary and that a new executive director had to be brought in. I also stepped down as the chair and Ramamurti took over this responsibility.

Another board member, Lord Amir Bhatia, who was earlier on the Board of Oxfam GB, suggested the name of Bharti Patel from the UK. She had experience in advocacy work for the voluntary sector there. After a telephonic interview, the decision was made to appoint Bharti Patel as executive director. I gave her considerable support for the six years she was head, but she did not quite deliver. She had a very limited understanding of the conditions and problems in India and could not garner enough cooperation from the staff, which had become sizeable as a result of the SIDA grant. Bharti also had certain personal interests to attend to in her ancestral village. After Bharti, Mohan Prabhu was appointed, and she was supposed to mentor him before leaving. That did not work out either and a professor at IIM Bangalore, Vasanthi Srinivasum, took over as the chair.

Dr Parsuraman, an anthropologist and director of Tata Institute of Social Sciences, and Dr Sudarshan Iyer were among the important members of the Board. During this time, I proposed that instead of supporting project work and advocacy, the emphasis should be on identifying and nurturing creative people for radical change through a programme of Svaraj Fellowships. Here I had in mind the earlier experience with Ashoka Fellowships, but with a value framework that was Swaraj-ist. This would involve the Svaraj Fellows working closely with local communities, helping them to deepen an understanding of their situation and their resources for development, as well as resistance in a sustainable manner. I also felt that Vasanthi, Sudarshan Iyengar and Parsuraman, with the considerable intellectual resources at their disposal, could provide mentoring support to the fellows.

We held a series of meetings to define the outline of the idea. There was broad agreement, but without deeper understanding and commitment. Svaraj carried on for a while, but soon became untenable and a decision was made to close it down.

Another area of my involvement was, and continues to be, the mentoring of young persons with an urge to do something for society and to live their lives more creatively and purposefully. This is a very long list—I cannot even remember the names of all the people who came along with their questions and ideas. My role was mainly to listen to them and to understand their motivation and commitment. I shared my experience and what had led me to become engaged in public life and the voluntary sector. I can mention three to four names as an example: Manish Jain of Shikshantar and Swaraj University, Ravi Badri of Ekta Parishad and his wife Priya, Vipul Shaha and, of course, Mihir Bharadwaj and Mackenzie Shreve. For me, personally, these were all experiences of reviving hope in the generally bleak and despairing situation of the world around us.

From time to time, old and new friends have dropped in with a similar purpose, like Vijay Pratap and Rajni Bakshi from Lokayan days, Medha Patkar from the Narmada Bachao Andolan, and more recently, Kumar Prashant and Sudhir Chandra, Aseem Shrivastava, Ashish Kothari and Dr Sheikh Ghulam Hussein, and the late Kamla Bhasin.

14

My Tryst with Gandhi

'ज़िक्र जम्मू का, बात गांधी की
ताब ताम्बे का, चाल आँधी की!'

('Memories of Jammu, conversations about Gandhi;
Rage burning like burnished copper, sweeping through like
hot winds.')[1]

4 August 1947 ke din Gandhi Srinagar se laut rahe hain. Jammu sheher se baahar ubar–khaabar maidan mein bheed unn tak intezaar kar rahi hai. Iss din ke apne dispatch mein The Hindu *ke patrkaar ne iska byora inn shabdon mein diya hai:*

(On 4 August 1947, Gandhi returned from Srinagar. He was to stay in Jammu overnight. Beyond the city of Jammu, crowds gathered at the patchy, uneven maidan, awaiting his arrival. This is how a correspondent of *The Hindu* described the event:)

> Awaiting his arrival was a great concourse of people, who had all been standing around, sitting and talking, and craning their eyes up the road expecting him to arrive at any moment. Every time a vehicle was sighted in the distance, cheers of greeting would go up in the air. Then disappointment would ensue. The police had a hard time controlling the eager throng. At long last the motorcade arrived. As it drew to a halt Gandhiji emerged.
>
> A police official advised him to drive on in his car right up to the side of the dais. But Gandhji waved him aside. Breaking his day long silence, he said, 'The crush is too great, safety always lies in walking.' Proving the

point he soon walked through the crowd and reached the dais in only five minutes.[3]

Mai uss bheed mein maujud thha. Meri yaddaasht kuchh alag hai. Bheed itni nahi thhi. Der hone ke kaaran log bikhar gaye thhe. Maine Gandhi-ji ko manch ki ore jaate hue nazdeek se dekha. Do sahaayikaon ke kandhon par haath rakhe ve manch ki ore jaa rahe thhe. Surya ast hote samay apni divya lalima mein chamak raha thha aur uske saamne Gandhi-ji ki deh taambe ki tarah damak rahi thhi. Kaun kis ko abha de raha thha, kehna kathin hai! Saanjha ki bela, prarthana ka samay. Gandhi manch se dheemi awaaz mein kuchh keh rahe thhe par mere aaspaas khadhe logon mein unhe sunne mein utsaah nahi thha. Ve Pakistan hone waale Punjab se ujdhe sharanaarthi thhe jo Gandhi ko apni durdasha ke liye doshi maante thhe. Mai bhi unmein se ek thha jo apne 15th saal mein, Rawalpindi se nikla, na unko samajh paa raha thha, na Gandi ki ore na apne aap ki. Parantu—

Unn dekhne aur nakaarne ke kshanon mein kuchh aisa hua jis ne abhi tak mujhe Gandhi se jodhe rakha hai. Iss rishte ki alag kahaani hai.

(I was part of that assembly. My recollections are a little different. The crowd wasn't large, since the programme had been delayed and many had left. That's why I got a glimpse of Gandhi advancing towards the stage up close. His hands were on the shoulders of his two women helpers. The sun was setting and the sky had an ineffable glow. Gandhi's skin gleamed like copper. It was difficult to say who was endowing grace upon whom! It was dusk and Gandhi's time for prayer. His voice was gentle, but those who were around me were not too keen to listen. They blamed him for the plight of refugees displaced from West Punjab. I was one of them as well, only 15 years old, a refugee from Rawalpindi and unable to understand either the people around me, or Gandhi, or myself.

Even so, in that moment of beholding and negating, something transpired that so moved me that Gandhi became a central figure in my life. However, that is a story for another day.)[3]

My next exposure to Gandhi was in 1959, through the book *A Saint on the March* (1956) by Hallam Tennyson, which describes the author's experience of walking with Gandhian activist Vinoba Bhave during the Bhoodan/Gramdaan movement. As I mentioned in Chapter 3, after reading the book I could not sleep for three nights. A constant refrain rang in my head: 'You should be there', meaning that I should be in that movement. But that was not to be since I had to serve Kenya's government for three years after my studies on state scholarship. Eventually the storm subsided and routine took over. But something remained, to be revived after my return to India in 1972.

During this time, I was also neighbours with the Gujarati family of Doctor S. B. Gaur. There were intermittent conversations about Gandhi and I remember the visit of a Gandhian, Indulal Yagnik, who was a prominent leader of the movement for the separate state of Gujarat. Later, during a visit to India in 1964–65 with my wife, I visited Sevagram and met the Gandhians Aryanakam and his wife Ashadevi, who were active in introducing Nai Talim. Before that, in 1961–62, I lived as a paying guest in Birmingham with the political scientist/sociologist Geoffrey Ostergaard. He was engaged in the study of the Gandhian movement in India after Gandhi. Over meals, we sometimes talked about Gandhi, although I did not have much knowledge about him or the movements he had led.

As a student in Birmingham University, I also had the chance to talk to a group of post-graduate students studying there, but they were mostly in engineering and not greatly concerned with Gandhi's ideas. Later, in 1968, when we moved from Kenya to the USA to work with Friends World College, I discovered that the spirit and influence of Gandhi had moved to the United States through the civil rights movement led by Martin Luther King, Jr. There I took part in various peace movements and critiques of the prevailing systems in the West, including the one-million-strong Washington peace march in 1969. In 1971, during my visit to Mexico with the student group from FWC, I led a seminar based on Erik Erikson's book, *Gandhi's Truth* (1969). During my time with Friends/Quakers, I had the opportunity to witness the working of the principles of peace and harmony in practice.

On our return to India in 1972, I once again visited Sevagram for a national conference on education inaugurated by the Prime Minister, Indira Gandhi. In my work as director of Vidya Bhawan Rural Institute, I studied and tried to revive the ideas of community development and panchayati raj, which owed their inspiration to Gandhi. During the 1970s, an attempt was made to develop an interface between voluntary organisations and the Gandhian movement led by Jayaprakash Narayan. I took part in one of the seminars organised by JP Narayan's associate Ranjit Gupta and presented a paper on 'The catalyst role of voluntary organizations—the Gandhian imperative'. In Udaipur in the 1970s, there was an active tradition of Gandhian work, led by Deen Dayal Dashottar, Dayal Chand Soni, Bhurelal Baya and others. Vidya Bhawan had started a school based on Gandhi's 'Basic Education' in 1941, headed by Dayal Chand Soni, but like the VB Rural Institute, it had to make compromises with the main educational system. This considerably weakened the Basic Education thrust.

Seva Mandir and its founder, Dr Mohan Singh Mehta, had an ambiguous attitude to Gandhi, his thought and his work. On the one hand, they recognised his greatness and contribution to India's freedom and to communal harmony, as well as his commitment to ahimsa (non-violence) and peace. However, in the post-independence scenario, they went along the path charted by the Congress under Nehru's leadership. At the national level, I began to attend the conferences of Sarva Seva Sangh and Sarvodaya Samaj. I also worked with Radhakrishna, secretary of Gandhi Peace Foundation, on some initiatives in constructive work.

The 1970s was a time of crisis in the Sarvodaya movement, with differences between Vinoba Bhave and Jayaprakash Narayan. As a result, there was a split in the movement. I found myself on the side of those who supported JP. Overall, however, I remained on the margins of this movement. A closer involvement was with the interface of the Gandhian movement and the environment movement, in which the leaders of the Chipko Movement, Chandi Prasad Bhatt and Sundarlal Bahuguna, were prominent figures. They took an active interest in the environment protection work we had begun in the Aravallis. I met another Gandhian leader and associate of Vinoba Bhave in the Bhoodan Movement, Vimla Thakar, and had the opportunity to accompany her team for a peace mission in Punjab during the Khalistan movement there.

As I have described earlier, during my involvement with Lokayan I took part in a seminar aimed at taking a fresh look at Gandhi's *Hind Swaraj*. I presented a paper titled 'Gandhian Frame of Action', which was later published as a part of the proceedings of the seminar. I also arranged a dialogue between Rajni Kothari—the key figure in Lokayan and Founder/Director of the Centre for the Study of Developing Societies—and Gandhian leaders Sidhhraj Dhadda, Thakurdas Bang, Govind Rao Deshpande and N. Krishnaswamy. This was a disappointing experience as both sides talked past each other without listening to one another. I also worked with the Association of Voluntary

Agencies in Rural Development (AVARD), set up by JP for coordinating voluntary effort in rural development.

During the 1980s, my major involvement by far was in the environment movement. As I have written earlier, it began during my work in Seva Mandir in the 1970s, where I introduced soil and water conservation activities through watershed development on degraded lands as a part of the work of the organisation. This led to my realisation that extensive damage had been done to the hilly areas of the Aravallis due to the deforestation of the past two to three decades. This created a sense of personal crisis, which culminated in my leaving Seva Mandir. I have already written about the beginnings of my work with Ubeshwar Vikas Mandal and its engagement in the wasteland development programme of the Government of India.

ENDNOTES

1. Translated into English by Alok Bhalla.

2. Ramamurthy, Vaidyanathan. 2003. *From the Pages of The Hindu: Mahatma Gandhi—The Last 200 Days*: 43–44. The Hindu Group.

3. Translated into English by Alok Bhalla.

Afterword

I would like to conclude these memoirs with some reflections on remembering and living, followed by a summing up and assessment of my own life as depicted in the previous chapters. Looking back over seven decades of my life and work, I ask myself, what do they add up to?

To paraphrase Urdu writer Intezar Hussein's observation in '*Kahani to awara hoti hai*', translated by Alok Bhalla as 'Story is a Vagabond', I would say that 'Memories are vagabonds'— '*yaadein aawara hoti hain*'. In this mood, my thoughts about memories can be crystallised as a Punjabi ditty:

यादां...
Yaadan…

यादां इ यादां
Yaadan ee yaadan

यादा चार छपेरै घुमन
Yaadan char chhapere ghuman

यादां उगन यादां डुबन
Yaadan ugan yaadan duban

यादां कट्टन यादां चुमन
Yaadan kattan yaadan chumman

यादां डसन यादां हस्सन
Yaadan dassan yaadan hassan

यादां दियां नइं मर्यादां
Yaadan diyaan nahin maryaadan

यादां नूं की फ़रयादां
Yaadan nu ki faryaadan

यादां इ यादां
Yaadan ee yaadan

Memories…
Memories upon memories
Memories wander in all directions
Memories sprout, memories sink
Memories bite, memories caress
Memories sting, memories laugh
Memories know no limits
No use pleading with memories
Memories upon memories

More prosaically, memoirs can be written as autobiography, fiction, confessions, or as the Gandhian innovation, *Atma Katha—The Story of My Experiments with Truth*. As it turns out, my own memoirs, as an attempt to impose some order on their '*aawargi*', their randomness, have taken shape as a combination of autobiography, social history and a chronicle of my efforts in public work.

As autobiography, the memoirs depict my growth from a callow youth to a professional with a sense of vocation, to a caring family man, to a responsible citizen, and finally, to an aged but self-reflexive mentor.

As social history, they describe life in segregated, colonial Kenya, then its post-independence transition and integration. They go on to depict academic life and culture in a 'Red Brick' university as well as Oxford in postwar England. This is interspersed with glimpses of life and culture amidst the colonial Indian communities and their educational institutions in Kenya. The memoirs then shift to the libertarian, radical educational experiment in the revolutionary 1960s in the USA.

My return to India is marked by glimpses of life and culture in traditional Mewar society, gradually adapting to and adopting development and modernisation. Likewise, there are depictions of voluntarism and voluntary institutions undergoing change, from selfless service efforts to professional, bureaucratic entities and later to social enterprises.

My involvement in public work is a narrative of my activities—as an educator both in formal institutional settings and independently; as a social worker working in relief, poverty alleviation and community-based development; and as an activist in campaigns for social justice and environmental protection and regeneration.

Finally, whether my life as depicted in these memoirs, especially my involvement in public life, has been worthwhile, it is for the reader to judge. For me, it has been gratifying to discover early a sense of vocation as a teacher/educator, followed by my awakening, as a student of geography, to the world reality with its remarkable and complex functioning. This was followed by a realisation that the world at this juncture was in a state of crisis created by modern human civilisation. The responsibility to address this situation also lay with human agency and one had to play a part in this venture as an intellectual and as an activist. Living along this threefold trajectory, I have reached the end of the ninth decade of my life, a constant source of wonder and astonishment. What lies ahead and for how long, is not for me to say. However, for as long as life lasts, I wish that hope and effort will be sustained. इति!